HAWAI'I
NEI

∿

TALANOA: CONTEMPORARY PACIFIC LITERATURE

HAWAI'I NEI

NEI

~

ISLAND

PLAYS

VICTORIA NALANI KNEUBUHL

University of Hawai'i Press

HONOLULU

07 06 05 04 03 02   6 5 4 3 2 1

Library of Congress Cataloging-in-Publication Data

Kneubuhl, Victoria N. (Victoria Nalani)
Hawai'i nei : island plays / Victoria Nalani Kneubuhl.
   p. cm. — (Talanoa)
The conversation of Ka'ahumanu — Emmalehua —Ola na iwi.
ISBN 0–8248–2539–X (pbk. : alk. paper)
   1. Hawaii—Drama. I. Title. II. Series.

PS3561.N418 H39 2002
812'.54—dc21

                                        2002018081

University of Hawai'i Press books are printed on acid-free paper
and meet the guidelines for permanence and durability of
the Council on Library Resources.

Printed by Versa Press, Inc.

CONTENTS

ACKNOWLEDGMENTS

Like the production of a play, the publication of a book is the work of many hands.

My endless thanks are extended to the Center for Biographical Research at the University of Hawai'i at Mānoa for its commitment to this project, and to its director, Craig Howes, whose guidance, direction, and indefatigable energy made this volume of plays a reality. My kind thanks also to Stan Schab for his text design and for liking the birds.

I am indebted to the University of Hawai'i Press for its support of my work, and in particular to Pam Kelly for initiating the process of publication. I would also like to offer my heartfelt thanks to my editor, Masako Ikeda, for her sensitive help and support in carrying this project through.

Words of gratitude are also sent out to Barbara Pope for her elegant design work, and to Annie Rogers for making me look good.

I would also gratefully acknowledge three institutions that have consistently supported my work and growth as a theatre artist: Kumu Kahua Theatre, Honolulu Theatre for Youth, and the Department of Drama and Theatre at the University of Hawai'i at Mānoa.

Certain individuals have given of themselves to help make me a playwright. I will always thank my teacher Dennis Carroll for nurturing me as a writer, and for having confidence in my work before I was able to find my own. Thanks to my special sisters in theatre, Juli Burk and Pam Sterling, for their generous help in reading, encouraging, and directing my work.

For emotional, material, and every other kind of support, I thank Philip D. Haisley, Jr. For listening to and understanding a dramatic personality, I thank Mary Hogan, and for knowing a good play when he sees one, I thank Nikolai Buchholz.

Finally, my humble thanks to all the actors, directors, readers, designers, technicians, theatre office workers, and theatre audiences who have, over the years, come together to give life and meaning to these plays.

INTRODUCTION

CRAIG HOWES

Victoria Nalani Kneubuhl was born in 1949. Her father's side of the family is Samoan, German, Swiss, and Welsh. Her mother's side is English, Irish, and Hawaiian. A royalist, Kneubuhl's great grandmother lived and died devoted to Hawai'i's last monarch, the overthrown Queen Lili'uokalani.

After finishing her B.A. in Hawaiian Cultural Studies, Art, and Psychology through Antioch University in 1982, Kneubuhl began taking playwriting courses at the University of Hawai'i at Mānoa in 1983, receiving an M.A. in Drama and Theatre in 1987. Her training in Hawaiian cultural history and theatre later proved invaluable at the Hawai'i Mission Houses Museum, where from 1987 to 1990 she was Coordinator of Educational Programs and then Curator of Education, and at the Judiciary History Center of Hawai'i, where from 1990 to 1993 she was an Education Specialist. At first a tour leader and a role player in the Mission Houses Living History project, she was soon researching and writing the grants and scripts for such programs as *In Our Own Words,* her 1990 compilation of letters, journals, and compositions of nineteenth-century Hawaiian and missionary women. For the Judiciary History Center, she drew on court transcripts to produce two dramatic recreations of landmark Hawai'i trials. *Duncan v. Kahanamoku* (1992) concerned the imposition of martial law and the suspension of habeas corpus during World War II. *Trial of a Queen* (1995) commemorated the 100th anniversary of the 1895 Military Tribunal that charged Lili'uokalani with treason against those who had overthrown her.

Kneubuhl's most ambitious staging of pivotal historical moments was *January 1893,* a five-act, nineteen scene, fifteen-hour-long "living history pageant" which Dennis Carroll has called "the most significant recent local-Hawaiian theatre event to dramatize the loss felt in the present by the 'crimes' of the past" (140). Produced as part of *'Onipa'a,* the centennial observance of the overthrow of the Hawaiian monarchy, and with individual scenes often taking place on the exact location and date of the represented event, *January 1893* was seen in whole or part by between 10,000 and 20,000 people. In 1998 came *The Annexation Debate,* a living history presentation commissioned to mark the centennial of Hawai'i's absorption into the United States.

Kneubuhl has also drawn on oral history for her live and video-taped dramatic works. In *Getting Somewheres* (1996), the plantation experiences of Hawai'i's women are presented in their own words. Performed at least 170 times, it was adapted for television in 1998, as part of Hawai'i Public Television's *Spectrum* series. *Into the Marketplace: Working-Class Women in 20th Century Hawai'i* (1995) explores the difficulties encountered by women entering the workforce. Kneubuhl's most ambitious video project has been *The Great Hawaiian Dock Strike* (1999). Broadcast as part of HPT's *Rice and Roses* series, this hour-long production blended archival film, photographs, audio clips, interviews with the participants, and living history dramatizations to commemorate the fiftieth anniversary of a crucial moment in Hawai'i's labor history.

Kneubuhl has written a number of plays in addition to the three in this collection. Almost all have been produced at least once. Written for a course in playwriting in 1983, her first play, the one-act *Veranda Dance,* was produced at the University of Hawai'i at Mānoa in 1986. Its non-realistic staging, and its focus on a young woman's entrapment within socially-sanctioned roles, foreshadowed her later full-length play The *Story of Susanna* (1998). A number of plays deal with Samoa, where Kneubuhl lived for years. *Manusina* (1988) explores three generations of women, all struggling to reconcile, or to choose between, the strengths and obligations of Samoan culture and the attractions and costs of modernization and introduced western values. *Tofa Samoa* (1992), a Honolulu Theatre for Youth production, toured Hawai'i in 1994. And *Ola Nā Iwi* and *Fanny and Belle,* both discussed below, feature Samoan characters and settings.

Though women's issues and the interplay between past and present remain constants in her work, Kneubuhl has recently ventured into new settings. *The Story of Susanna* uses the apocryphal account of Susanna and the Elders to examine current social expectations about women, and the consequences, sometimes violent, that arise from resisting these expectations. Poetic sequences alternate with naturalistic scenes in women's halfway houses. Dance and choral work pervade the narrative. Three public readings, begun in 1996, were followed by its first production at the University of Hawai'i at Mānoa in 1998, and a reading that same year at Washington, D.C.'s Arena Stage. Later published in *Seventh Generation: An Anthology of Native American Plays* (1999), *The Story of Susanna* was produced at Bowling Green State University in 2001 and at the University of North Dakota in 2002.

Kneubuhl's most recent play, *Fanny and Belle,* examines the relationship between the mother-and-daughter historical figures Fanny Stevenson and Isobel Strong. As husband and stepfather to these women, Robert Louis Stevenson is an important figure in the play, but the conflicts and reconciliations between these two women over the course of Fanny's long life are Kneubuhl's main concerns. As the setting for much of *Fanny and Belle's* second act, Samoa also returns to a prominent place in her writing. The play has not yet been produced; it received a staged reading at Kumu Kahua Theatre in 1999, and an Honorable Mention in the Bay Area Playwriting Festival.

Kneubuhl's best known dramatic works, however, deal with Hawaiian subjects. With Ryan Page, Robert Nelson, and Dennis Carroll, she co-authored *Ka'iulani: A Cantata for Theatre* (1987), a play about the brief life of the last designated heir to the throne. This drama and *The Conversion of Ka'ahumanu* were the plays performed on Kumu Kahua Theatre's 1990s International Tour to Edinburgh, Scotland, Washington, D.C., and Los Angeles. Two plays produced by Honolulu Theatre for Youth also represent Hawai'i's past and current challenges. *Paniolo Spurs* (1994) introduces children to the culture and traditions of the Hawaiian cowboy, while *Ka Wai Ola: The Living Waters* (1998) explores contemporary issues surrounding access to Hawaiian water.

Victoria Kneubuhl has been frequently honored for her work. The American Association of State and Local History gave *January 1893* its Award of Merit. The *Honolulu Star-Bulletin* named her one of the "10 Who Made a Difference" for 1993. Invited to be one of the eight featured artists at the 1994 Pacific Writers Forum, in that same year she received the Hawai'i Heritage Center Keeper of the Past Award. In 1996, the Hawai'i State Foundation for Culture and the Arts granted her an Individual Artist Fellowship; in 1999, she was invited to serve as a Community Scholar in the Colleges of Arts and Sciences, University of Hawai'i at Mānoa. And in 1994, she received the Hawai'i Award for Literature, the highest honor the state bestows upon a writer.

Victoria Kneubuhl continues to work in a variety of genres, with print, stage, and video projects planned for well into the future.

VICTORIA KNEUBUHL AS A PLAYWRIGHT

Claiming that she began writing "only by accident," Victoria Kneubuhl was in her early thirties when she completed her first play. Theatre had not been a big part of her life. Before taking her first playwriting class in 1983, she had seen "maybe five plays," and her acting experience had been confined to *The Brave Bears of Lahore,* a play staged as part of a Honolulu Theatre for Youth summer program she attended when she was eight. Yet she did come from what could be called a theatrical family, because her uncle was the playwright and screenwriter John Kneubuhl. A central figure in Hawai'i's theatre community in the 1940s and 1950s, Kneubuhl wrote for major Hollywood television series in the 1950s and 1960s, then taught and wrote plays in Samoa during the 1970s. It's hardly surprising, then, that when his niece found all the university fiction writing courses closed, she rationalized signing up for a playwriting class by thinking "Oh yeah, my uncle does that."

John Kneubuhl had more effect on her choice of subjects and her understanding of theatre than on the actual structure and dialogue of her plays. His "really big personality" and his strong notions about what made a play good or bad were too overpowering for a beginning playwright, and so at least when it came to the nuts-and-bolts of writing, she decided "not to be around him." Sharing his sense of artistic mission, however, was another matter. John Kneubuhl believed deeply that Pacific cultural material was a rich resource for the theatre, and that as a Polynesian dramatist, his duty was to translate and create, and not to appropriate. He wrote about the Pacific as a Samoan, just as his niece would write as a Hawaiian-Samoan. He also felt that theatre has an important function within the community. Since drama as an art form is a medium for exploring serious issues, a playwright must stay away from "the campy kind of entertainment showbiz part of theatre." Victoria Kneubuhl credits her uncle with teaching her that "It's better to flop on your face trying to do something that has some integrity than to write crowd pleasers so you can hear people applauding for them." Put another way, uncle and niece agreed that "we didn't want to paint Red Skelton clowns."

This aesthetic meshed perfectly with the environment she found in her courses at the university. A beginning playwriting class with Bernard Dukore was followed by a class with Dennis Carroll. Carroll had impressive credentials as a scholar, teacher, and director, and fifteen years earlier he had co-founded Kumu Kahua Theatre, a company devoted to producing plays about life in Hawai'i, by Hawai'i's playwrights, for Hawai'i's people. The first play Kneubuhl wrote for Carroll, the one-act *Veranda Dance,* received a student production three years later. It was however her first full-length play, *Emmalehua,* that not only initiated her important artistic relationship with Kumu Kahua, but also established what she has called the "unbroken connection with Pacific island life as the rich well-spring" which inspires her work (Gilbert 364).

The mid-to-late 1980s were important years in the development of a Hawai'i theatre, with Kneubuhl's plays contributing greatly to this process. In his essay "Hawai'i's 'Local' Theatre," Dennis Carroll draws on the work of Jonathan Okamura to suggest that the political, economic, and social environment during this period provoked responses from two kinds of dramatists—"Hawaiian indigenous" playwrights, and "local" playwrights, generally of Asian ancestry, whose families had arrived in Hawai'i as part of its plantation history. Quoting Okamura, Carroll argues that these writers share "an appreciation of and a commitment to the islands and their peoples, cultures and ways of life." But further, as Hawai'i increasingly becomes "dominated by multinational corporations and market forces over which the people of the islands really have no control," these dramatic writers find Hawai'i's future less and less promising (123).

Although Okamura notes that native Hawaiians can "without contradiction" claim both local and indigenous identities, Carroll uses Kneubuhl's plays as examples of a distinctly Hawaiian theatre. Such works often dramatize the conflicts and compromises between "Hawaiian culture and the world of the emergent missionary and commercial-American class that suborned it." Often historical, these plays will use Hawaiian language, hula, and chant when exploring the roots of "loss and cultural dispossession," although contemporary scenes may employ pidgin (Hawaiian Creole English) as well. "Surreal stylization" is also a common strategy for undermining narrative conventions which might reinforce the political or social status quo (125). Or as former UH Theatre Professor Juli Burk once remarked when describing Kneubuhl's work, "the plays share non-realistic structures, as events are interwoven rather than presented in linear progression, and stories unfold rather than develop." Burk went on to stress the importance of gender in Kneubuhl's work, noting that "larger issues" of acculturation, assimilation, and racism are explored in the plays "through the lived experience of their central female characters, who survive through integrating their cultural heritage with the necessities of their contemporary existence."

The challenges Kneubuhl faced in writing such plays, and Kumu Kahua faced in staging them, were often formidable. In Hawai'i, the universal difficulty of attracting audiences to original plays was compounded by widespread cultural assumptions that art came from elsewhere. "I'll never forget this woman asking me 'Have you been in any plays?'" Kneubuhl recalls. "I said, 'Oh yes, I've been in several Kumu Kuhua plays,' and the woman replied, 'No, I mean a real play.'" The local and the Hawaiian communities could be skeptical as well. Since the Pacific has so frequently been misinterpreted in "some pretty kitchy and campy and stereotypical ways," Kneubuhl soon learned that people would get "really offended" at how their cultural and historical heritage was represented. Finally, the actors, directors, and the other specialists necessary for producing the plays were developing the methods for staging them at the same time that the dramatists were learning how to create them. As a result, when asked what was the biggest difficulty in writing Hawai'i plays in the mid '80s, "casting and directing" was Kneubuhl's immediate reply. "It was so hard to cast *Emmalehua*," she recalled, "We had to beg people to come and be in that play." In time, though, Kumu Kahua's commitment to producing works like Kneubuhl's changed the theatrical climate. When Dennis Carroll directed a new production of *Emmalehua* ten years later, "thirty people showed up for the auditions."

Artistic collaboration has shaped Kneubuhl's career in a number of ways. To begin with, her affiliations with Kumu Kahua and Honolulu Theatre for Youth have meant that a remarkably high number of her plays were produced almost from the moment she began writing. Kneubuhl herself believes this has influenced her profoundly, since a production is "the best teacher." Course due dates, commissions, and production deadlines have also stimulated her efforts, leading her to conclude that "sometimes working under the gun is good for you." Kumu Kahua Theatre compounded this pressure, because its commitment to developing as well as staging Hawai'i plays often meant that the manuscript had to move through several consulting stages. Kneubuhl recalls that after seeing a draft, the Artistic Director and board members "would say 'Oh, we want to have a reading,' so I was forced to fix my script up. And then they'd say, 'Oh, we want to produce it,' so then you have to write, because it's going to be out there."

Finally, because her first plays were composed when Kumu Kuhua did not have a permanent home, Kneubuhl found that when writing, she would "never imagine anything other than an open space loosely defined by a light." This indeterminacy proved to be an advantage.

Not only did directors and designers enjoy a greater degree of artistic freedom, but Kneubuhl also benefited from being forced to ground her plays in her chosen characters and cultural materials. "Every play has its own little life, and each of the different kinds of material that you start looking into has its own ecosystem," she believes. If you can keep yourself from locking this system down physically in place, "pretty soon, stuff just appears out of the material of its own self."

Here Kneubuhl points to an important quality of many recent plays dealing with local, Hawaiian, and Pacific issues. In Hawaiʻi theatre, the characters and the audience know that things are always developing—historical, cultural, economic things—in the outside world. Often the characters' experiences parallel or echo what has happened or is still happening outside. In some cases, though, the people or the events themselves come on stage. Kaʻahumanu or Liliha actually appear as characters, or other characters may reproduce the conflicts arising within the Hawaiian community over the repatriation and reburial of human remains, or within a family over the preservation of its traditional lands. In this way, Kneubuhl's plays are both local and Hawaiian in Carroll's sense. Acknowledged or not, the force of historical and cultural change presses on everyone living in Hawaiʻi. But for scores of reasons, this pressure is particularly intense upon native Hawaiians, and the theatre ideally can provide a parallel space for exploring the personal costs, the contradictions, and the resulting conflicts of living under this weight.

The three plays in this collection are products of a rich, energetic period in the ongoing collaborative efforts to develop and sustain a Hawaiʻi theatre. And they are also the works of a remarkably dedicated, accomplished, honored, and important playwright.

THE CONVERSION OF KAʻAHUMANU

I do not look to the past with contempt, but seek to preserve the ways that were good, uniting them with what is good of this new world, that comes to us now.

> — Kaʻahumanu, *The Conversion of Kaʻahumanu*

The Conversion of Kaʻahumanu has been Victoria Kneubuhl's most produced play. First staged by Kumu Kahua in 1988, the play was performed in Samoa that same year. In 1990 it toured Hawaiʻi, then traveled with *Kaʻiulani* to Edinburgh, Washington, D.C., and Los Angeles.

Since then, readings have been staged for fundraising events. The play has been published twice: in *But Still, Like Air, I'll Rise: New Asian American Plays* (1997), edited by Velina Hasu Houston, and in *Postcolonial Plays: An Anthology* (2001), edited by Helen Gilbert.

As Gilbert notes, both *Ka'iulani* and *The Conversion of Ka'ahumanu* focus "on legendary women of the Hawaiian royalty at pivotal moments in their kingdom's history." Unlike Ka'iulani, though, Ka'ahumanu (c. 1768–1832) wielded the power necessary to affect Hawai'i's history as it struggled to deal with the arrival of even greater powers. She was the favorite wife of Kamehameha I, who managed in the years following Western contact to draw all of the islands together under his authority. After his death in 1819, Ka'ahumanu assumed the role of *kuhina nui*, or regent, with responsibility for advising the new ruler Liholiho, now Kamehameha II, the son of Keōpūolani, the most highly born of Kamehameha I's wives. Two moments in Ka'ahumanu's remarkable life stand out as pivotal for Hawaiian history. First, by eating publicly in 1819 with Liholiho, she brought to an end the kapu system—that web of privileges, restrictions, and obligations that had ordered Hawai'i. Second, by converting in 1825 to Christianity, she essentially mandated what system should replace the one she had declared over. Set in the time between these events, Kneubuhl's play explores the consequences of this eventual shift for Ka'ahumanu, for her Hawaiian subjects, for the recently-arrived missionaries, and for the subsequent history of Hawai'i.

The Conversion is the product of a remarkable convergence of influences. After entering the graduate program in Theatre at the University of Hawai'i, Kneubuhl took a seminar on Women and Theatre offered by Juli Burk, and enrolled in a directed study with Dennis Carroll, which was designed to result in a full-length play. Kneubuhl was also working in the Mission Houses Museum's Living History program, which presented to the public fully costumed missionaries and their charges recreating the activities of a typical day in 1831. Since an adult of this time would of course be intimately familiar with the events of the preceding twenty years, improvising in character for hours each Saturday demanded that Kneubuhl and the other role players "had to know this material like we had lived it." This process of steeping herself in the historical period represented in *The Conversion* therefore made her far more familiar, both historically and dramatically, with her subject than most playwrights could ever hope to be.

All of the play's characters were anticipated in some way in this Living History program. One of the role players was Sybil Bingham, and Kneubuhl herself played Hannah Grimes, a character modeled on the historical Hannah Holmes. Since the Oahu missionaries would have known what was going on in Kona—and also because her journals were such a good source for historical information—the role players often talked about Lucy Thurston. Pali was not represented, nor did she have a historical counterpart, but the gossip often strayed to a similar "girl" serving another missionary. And although she never appeared, Ka'ahumanu was a constant topic of conversation. The Queen's actual rocking chair, made by Sybil Bingham's husband Hiram, was in the parlor where the Living History presentations took place, and Ka'ahumanu's doings—where she was, what she had done recently—were of the greatest interest to everyone.

Not surprisingly, then, having "all that research done already before I ever sat down to write" made *The Conversion* "the easiest" of Kneubuhl's plays to compose. Not just the historical underpinnings, but the characters' conflicts were firmly in hand. "I didn't have to contrive problems for them," she recalls, since "real nineteenth century problems were already there." Months of improvising in public with other informed actors made the dialogue easier to write; Kneubuhl gratefully admits that "a lot of Sybil Bingham's character is based on Deborah Pope's interpretation." The biggest challenge was distilling this huge amount of historical information down to a two-hour format, but this too proved manageable. Choosing a few subjects and moments to focus on took some time, but "once I picked those issues it was pretty easy."

Kneubuhl's dramatic approach brought the troubled state of affairs in early nineteenth century Hawai'i together with the assumptions and strategies of contemporary feminist theatre. The historical circumstances were overwhelming. "It's one of the most difficult time periods in Hawaiian history," Kneubuhl remarks, "because things are changing so quickly, and so many people are dying." As she began constructing a play that would deal with this traumatic material, she found the works of such dramatists as Caryl Churchill and Louise Page very helpful. Making the entire cast female and aiming for an ensemble effect were two of the most obvious influences. (The time-honored question "Whose play is this?" was in this case not the one to ask.) But Kneubuhl also gave *The Conversion* the episodic structure British feminist playwrights have often employed for exploring women's ideas and issues. Instead of moving a central plot from beginning to end, *The Conversion* tells "five stories, where each of these women starts at Point A and ends at another point." Since each story "has its own little climactic point and its own little resolutions," Kneubuhl's most interesting task "became how you mix these stories, how they interweave with each other."

The eventual set design reflected the episodic, free-flowing nature of the script. "Three different little locations any place in the world" were all the play required—a decision not just resulting from Kneubuhl's familiarity with contemporary drama, but also from her growing experience with the realities of production. "By this time I'd learned that no matter what you wrote in the set and stage directions, a designer would probably come and change it," she recalls, "So less is always more." Kneubuhl was not however simply making a virtue of necessity, because the set's simplicity reinforced the play's dramatic strength. As she wrote, she found herself trying to discover the feeling of where each character was. Then "you take that feeling, and you try and put one or two things there"—a mat, a glass, some playing cards, a book— "that the feeling can attach itself to." The result, as Dennis Carroll has described it, is "a chamber-play apparatus on an intimate, spare, open stage, employing monologues and direct address" (135).

Another powerful point of contact between the Hawaiian material and feminist theatre conventions is the play's treatment of status. Juli Burk, who served as dramaturg for the first production, noted that the Hawaiian characters "represent three social classes from within the indigenous culture, each confronting acculturation and assimilation by western culture in distinctive ways." It is the interplay between the Hawaiian characters—and between the missionary characters, for that matter—that keeps the play from devolving into a "missionaries versus Hawaiians" dispute. Instead, as Burk remarks, *The Conversion* "clearly and fully poses a number of questions and asks the viewer to encounter the larger issues through the personal lives of women."

These "larger issues"—colonialism, religion, and gender, among others—are important and contentious ones for anyone interested in Hawaiian history and culture. Take for example gender. Helen Gilbert writes that *The Conversion*'s "finely nuanced account of interactions between the missionary wives and the Hawaiian women they seek to convert to Christianity suggests ways in which gender acts as a category that cuts across the discursive field of imperialism" (364). Certainly, many have seen Ka'ahumanu's striking down of the kapu system as a liberating act for women, and Gilbert notes that Ka'ahumanu, Hannah, and Pali all admire "the more appealing aspects of missionary Christianity: its emphasis on tolerance and good works, its provision of education, and its relative respect for women." At the same time, though, Kneubuhl puts on display "the sexual repression, cultural chauvinism and staunch gender hierarchies undergirded by Christianity" (365). It is probably fair, then, to suggest that at least in *The Conversion*, Kneubuhl raises the gender dynamics of her subject to ask hard questions about them, rather than to offer a final word.

This is also true about another of the play's central concerns: the actions of Ka'ahumanu, and their results. When Dennis Carroll describes her as having been "admired or reviled by different groups of Hawaiians," he is referring in part to strong audience opinions about whether the historical Ka'ahumanu saved or betrayed Hawaiians and their culture (135). Kneubuhl achieves what Carroll calls her "complex and even-handed" treatment by stressing the impossibility of the situation. Given the benefit of historical hindsight, she notes, "It's really easy to say 'Oh they should have done this.'" Instead, Kneubuhl tried to show that "being there at that time and having to make those decisions was really difficult." The circumstances were unimaginably harsh. When missionaries like Sybil Bingham and Lucy Thurston arrived, barely forty years after Western contact, "half the people were dead already." Nor does the play suggest that exchanging one faith for another will solve things. Noting the irony that Ka'ahumanu "disbanded the traditional religion only to accept a similarly prescriptive regime," Gilbert points to Kneubuhl's "clear-eyed estimation of Christianity's relative merits and weaknesses for a specific society at a given historical place and time" (366).

Without necessarily agreeing with Gilbert that Ka'ahumanu's "sense of survivalism is itself presented as authentically Hawaiian—most indigenous precisely when it is most syncretic" (366), it is I think fair to say that like the other plays in this volume, *The Conversion of Ka'ahumanu* presents us with characters trying to make decisions that they and others can live with at a time of profound and murderous change. Large parts of the culture have been lost; other parts are fading. Some things can perhaps be revived; others can be preserved. But still others must be transformed, or even abandoned, in the face of forces from elsewhere—bad, good, mixed, indifferent. What makes *The Conversion* so compelling is not simply its effect as a play, which Dennis Carroll identifies as "predominantly realistic in style" but free from "the simple empathy and identification that often goes with that form" (136). Nor does the play's force arise entirely from such remarkable vignettes as Ka'ahumanu's dream sequence, when disembodied, increasingly urgent voices beg and command her to stop the suffering of her people. Rather, it is Kneubuhl's success in finding for her characters such distinctive, yet nuanced, and even self-contradictory positions, firmly grounded in the historical moment, that makes *The Conversion of Kaʻahumanu* the absorbing, complex play it is.

EMMALEHUA

Listen. We live and some things just come. Things we cannot stop. It's like things choose us. . . . And you, you were chosen for something too.

— Kaheka, *Emmalehua*

Over the years, Victoria Kneubuhl's first full-length play has also gone through the greatest transformations—and restorations. *Emmalehua* began in Dennis Carroll's advanced playwriting class in 1984. "He started off things by saying 'Well, this class is going to separate the men from the boys,'" Kneubuhl recalls, "I was wondering how I would fit in there." She decided first that this play would be about Hawaiʻi. Further, it would be about hula, and more specifically, about the difference between its commercialized forms and its status as a Hawaiian cultural rite. This sacred dimension intrigued her as a writer. "I was really fascinated with what it means when your art is totally infused with religious beliefs," she recalls. Finally, hula provided Kneubuhl with a visually and musically dramatic way to explore Hawaiian culture's fortunes in the modern world. She was reading a lot of Hawaiian history at the time—David Malo, Samuel Kamakau—and as a child she had been mesmerized by the stories she heard which testified to the power of Hawaiian spirits—the "things that would happen when promises were made and then they were broken, or when someone was made kapu, and the kapu's not lifted."

These interests all come together in the play's title character. Through Emma, Kneubuhl represents the spiritual dimensions of hula in Hawaiian culture, and also "the whole idea of kapu and sacredness, and what it would be like to actually be kapu." The play's Native American components, embodied in Adrian Clearwater, arose from other interests Kneubuhl was pursuing at the time. "I was reading something like *Black Elk Speaks*," she recalls, "it was the first time I really realized that certain indigenous cultures had things in common." In this case, Adrian and Emma are drawn together because they share an awareness of the spiritual dimensions lying beneath their daily activities in a modern America devoted to speed, force, development, and profit.

By setting *Emmalehua* in 1951, Kneubuhl intensifies all of the cultural conflicts at the same time as she makes them personal. The scene is the Hawai'i of her own childhood, which she looked back at from the 1980s with puzzlement and anger. After fifty years, the territorial government's steadfast support of a plantation economy was beginning to show major cracks, as first and second generation workers, primarily of Hawaiian, Chinese, Japanese, and Filipino ancestry, began to unionize and organize politically. The imposition of martial law after the bombing of Pearl Harbor in 1941—a control the military gave up reluctantly only near the end of the war—froze wages, suspended civil liberties, interned Japanese community leaders, and kept a tight control over any political dissent. At the same time, the thousands of Hawai'i residents from plantation backgrounds serving in America's armed forces became passionately certain that they were not fighting in Europe and the Pacific merely to protect the predominantly white oligarchy of agricultural, shipping, and mercantile interests who governed the territory. Almost immediately after these soldiers came home, the unions became extremely active and confrontational, staging major agricultural and dockyard strikes in the late 1940s. The territorial authorities and business leaders responded with laws that restricted, or even banned union activity, and with charges that the popular movement leaders were communists.

Two aspects of this struggle had a profound impact on Hawai'i's people during the 1950s: a renewed pressure to assume enthusiastically an American identity, and the steady shift towards a tourist economy. The many restrictions on constitutional rights that Hawai'i's territorial status made possible—martial law, a Washington-appointed rather than a popularly-elected governor—often led island-born residents to insist that they were not Japanese, Chinese, or Filipinos, but Americans, and therefore fully entitled to the benefits and freedoms enjoyed by their fellow citizens on the mainland. Often organizing along labor and war veteran lines, and not without heated conflicts, these groups coalesced into the state Democratic Party. Ten years after the war's end, this coalition controlled the territorial legislature; five years after that, Hawai'i had become the fiftieth state.

These gains accelerated changes already occurring in the economy. Put bluntly, those born on plantations did not want their children working on one, and at least at first, tourism's potential need for huge numbers of service workers, for private contracting and construction firms, and for strong civic and state support to maintain the infrastructure, made the visitor industry an attractive alternative to the

sugar and pineapple fields, and a means for securing outside invest-
ment less under the influence of those companies controlled by the
haole (white) oligarchy. Development became the goal, and for those
who were successful, a middle class lifestyle, complete with a house in
the suburbs and a one-income household, seemed possible.

Over the course of the century, these developments caught the
Hawaiian community up in a net of contradictory and perplexing
demands. When the monarchy was overthrown in 1893 by a tiny
group of predominantly white businessmen and professionals with
American military support, the nineteenth century's missionary injunc-
tions to exchange idolatry for a true religion became a government-
mandated suppression of Hawaiian language and culture as potential
sources of political dissent. Wrong and right became equated with past
and future. Looking forward meant looking toward America; looking
back would perpetuate poverty and superstition, and lead ultimately
to extinction. And yet, certain aspects of Hawaiian culture had been
commodified for tourist consumption long before World War II.
Dancing, singing, surfing, and cooking Hawaiians were essential to
the visitor industry—a guarantee, offered by the native people themselves, that a laid back, accepting, generous, and genial spirit pervaded
this American territory—the Aloha spirit. The postwar period only
accelerated this process, as tourism became the engine for escaping
Hawai'i's colonial past, and the children of the plantations became the
managers, workers, and supporters of an industry that marketed the
image of an attractive and welcoming Hawaiian to distinguish the
islands from other warm-weather destinations. Hawaiians were therefore encouraged to accept their own insignificance, to abandon or sup-
press much of their cultural inheritance, but to perform the role of
happy, culturally distinct natives before outsiders, and on demand.

Though 1951 was a year of rapid political and economic change,
then, it also appeared to be a low point for Hawaiian culture, and especially for hula. In school, Kneubuhl recalls, "people were really encouraged to be good little Americans." The elementary texts contained an
ideal environment of New England snow scenes, presented as somehow
more "real" than what lay outside the door. Since life apparently "takes
place somewhere else," the children found themselves encouraged to
think of Hawai'i as "some sort of shadowland." Local circles as well as
the larger world seemed to place little value on being Hawaiian, nor was
Hawaiian culture pointed to as a source of pride or self-esteem. This
"disconnected way of growing up and being educated" has clearly hurt
Emma's husband Alika, "whose vision of Hawai'i," as Juli Burk notes,
"encapsulates the American dream of economic expansion within a

homogenous Western society." But as the play opens, Emma herself is struggling "to abandon a personal and collective past of artistry and rich Hawaiian spirituality." It is her failure to do so that drives the play's narrative, and ultimately proves to be Emma's triumph.

When Kneubuhl submitted a draft of *Emmalehua* to Dennis Carroll, he urged her to develop it for production. He arranged for Kumu Kahua Theatre to give the play its first public reading in 1984. A number of drafts and revisions followed, with the first full production, directed by John Kneubuhl, taking place in 1986. At this point the collaborative nature of the process became more difficult, as he radically changed the ending, and the characters' lines and motivations as well. Emma's devotion to hula and her heritage became far less admirable. Alika's vision of Hawai'i's future, and his impatience with Emma's beliefs, were far more sympathetically presented. In Victoria's later estimation, what resulted from John Kneubuhl's revisions "wasn't the play I wrote. It was his play." But respect for his achievements as a playwright and director—and her wish for family peace—kept her from contesting the changes at the time.

The 1996 version of *Emmalehua* published in this collection was a revision and a restoration. After ten years of acting, playwriting, and production experience, Kneubuhl was a great deal more confident as a dramatist. She added several scenes, expanded the role of the chorus, and developed the Clearwater character further. Most importantly, she restored her own sense of the characters' motivations, and her original ending. Early collaboration with Dennis Carroll, the director of the second production, heightened the dramatic impact as well. When Carroll proposed his idea of the dais as the central set piece, Kneubuhl's former work with him on *Ka'iulani* and on earlier plays made it relatively easy "to mesh the script" with this director's vision. The eventual work is in Juli Burk's words a "highly theatrical" piece that "incorporates elements of Hawaiian and Native American culture through dance, chant, story, and the use of poetry and lyricism."

Emmalehua is a striking example of the benefits and difficulties arising from the collaborative process that has shaped so many of Hawai'i's plays. Beginning as a class assignment, this work went through readings, revisions, productions, and more revisions, with strong, sometimes conflicting reactions and advice at every phase from instructors, directors, actors, technical staff, audiences, and even relatives. It is a difficult path to follow, but one that Kneubuhl has traveled frequently over the course of her career.

OLA NĀ IWI

We can't eat stones, Kawehi.
Can't we?
— Pua and Kawehi, *Ola Nā Iwi*

Commissioned by Kumu Kahua Theatre, *Ola Nā Iwi* (The Bones Live) received a public reading in the Spring of 1994, and was produced that Fall. The Pan Asian Repertory Theatre in New York held a staged reading in 1998, and a full production was part of the University of Hawai'i at Hilo's 1999–2000 theatre season. If *The Conversion of Ka'ahumanu* and *Emmalehua* were plays of the mid-1980s, *Ola Nā Iwi* was definitely a play of the '90s. Kneubuhl was a far more experienced dramatist, with *Tofa Samoa* (1992), *Just So Stories* (1993), and the massive pageant *January 1893* (1993) only recently produced. But Hawai'i had also changed. After a brief honeymoon following statehood in 1959, by the mid-1960s the national civil rights movement and the Vietnam War had called into question local confidence that equality was simply a matter of having elected representatives in Washington, D.C. More crucially for Kneubuhl's writing, many Hawaiian scholars, artists, and cultural practitioners, often working through the 1930s, 1940s, and 1950s with little encouragement, had also prepared the way for a revival of interest in and commitment to things Hawaiian which came to be known as the Hawaiian Renaissance. During the 1970s, a massive resurgence of hula, chant, language instruction, and music paralleled an increasingly public and effective political activism that responded to the bombing of the island of Kaho'olawe by the U.S. military, to the eviction of Hawaiians from public lands, to the state and federal governments' supposed stewardship of Hawaiian land and water, and to the unearthing and desecration of Hawaiian remains. Issues of native sovereignty, economic development, education, cultural preservation, environmental dangers, land stewardship, and the legacy of history were more widely, frequently, and heatedly debated. *Ola Nā Iwi* deals with many of these issues, while remaining steeped in the history of how Hawai'i's cultural politics have developed.

A number of experiences inspired Kneubuhl as she wrote. The first was a story she had been told years before by a haole woman, a fairly recent arrival to Hawai'i, who lived in an oceanside condominium. As this woman walked along the beach each day, she would pass a little cave. Water washed the sand in and out; for some reason it scared her to walk by. One day, she saw an old woman crouching next to the cave. "Come," the old woman said, "Come over here." As the haole woman approached, the old woman crept further back into the cave. "Come, come," she beckoned. Following the still-retreating figure, the haole woman crawled in. When she got to the back of the cave, she found that even though there was no way to escape, the old woman was gone. But a skeleton lay scattered on the sand—so the haole woman dug a hole and buried the bones. Kneubuhl credits this story with inspiring one of the play's main narrative strands. "What if we weren't taking care of the remains?" she wondered, "What if they came back, and were able to take care of themselves?" In *Ola Nā Iwi*, the answer to the last question is the character Nanea/Liliha.

A second narrative strand emerged during the Kumu Kahua International Tour in 1990. As Kneubuhl gazed into a display case containing Hawaiian artifacts in Edinburgh, Scotland, one object in particular "seemed really alive and glad to see me, and knew who I was." She knew the reason why. "Hawaiians believe objects are invested with a life—a real life, not a symbolic life," she remarks, "I think mana does exist—it's for real, and some of these things still have that." In *Ola Nā Iwi*, this moment gets transformed in three significant ways. First, it is moved to Germany. Second, the artifact becomes human remains. And third, Kawehi, unconsciously acting in concert with Liliha, manages to get the bones back to Hawai'i—and in the process sets off the plot.

The third narrative strand appeared when Kneubuhl was working as an Education Specialist at the Judiciary History Center. In the Center library, she came across Roger G. Rose's slim monograph *Reconciling the Past: Two Basketry Kā'ai and the Legendary Līloa and Lonoikamakahiki*. Kneubuhl was fascinated by the book, and especially with the photographs, which "some people think should never have been taken." So moved was she by these woven repositories for honored bones—they were "so striking and strange looking to me"—that the making of a *kā'ai* became part of the play. (In one of *Ola Nā Iwi*'s more prophetic aspects, shortly before the play's run, the actual *kā'ai* were removed from the Bishop Museum. Presumably they were taken to the island of Hawai'i.)

At the same time, Kneubuhl was reading the U.S. Senate hearings on the Native American Graves Protection and Repatriation Act (NAGPRA). Among the materials accompanying the testimony were nineteenth and twentieth century documents which showed how museums and private collectors rationalized their fervent searches for native remains. Since Kneubuhl was working in a museum at the time, acquisitions issues were familiar to her. But the notion of anyone "collecting bones and storing them," or of entering into "competitions for who could scoop up more human remains and shove them in their collection," seemed inconceivable to her, and especially because the proper disposition of the dead was "such an emotional issue for Hawaiians and other Pacific people," as well as for Native Americans. "It seems barbaric when you think about it," Kneubuhl remarks, "You'd never go and dig up Benjamin Franklin and put him in an exhibit case."

Given these various influences, it seems fair to conclude that *Ola Nā Iwi* is one of Kneubuhl's most topical plays. But it is also her most tonally varied and structurally complex work. And the most humorous—"I felt like people were always saying 'O God, your plays are so heavy,' so this is me lightening up." If *The Conversion* was the easiest play to write, *Ola Nā Iwi* proved to be the most enjoyable. "I wanted to write a play that was funny and serious at the same time," she recalls, "I thought people might listen to me more if the material wasn't so pointed." The narrative itself is complicated, but loose. Though *Ola Nā Iwi* has four times as much plot as almost any other Kneubuhl play, the episodic qualities are even more pronounced. "I know there's an awful lot of scenes," she admits, "but I'm a great fan of those complicated mystery plots," so "little detective stories" run through the play. Other themes are developed through counterpoint. First there are the collector vignettes, which Kneubuhl thought of as pointedly Brechtian episodes that provide an outrageous, roughly chronological history of "how and why these human remains ended up in these collections." Then there is the Samoan content, introduced through the character Fatu—the fulfillment of a long-running playful conversation between Kneubuhl and her uncle John about the adventures of a fictional Samoan detective. *Ola Nā Iwi* also plays with the nature of drama itself. Some of the major characters are theatre people. Many impersonations and misrepresentations take place, culminating in the surreal costume party scene. And almost every character in the play is engaged in some version of director Erik's brooding attempts to arrange and block out the course of events.

Finally, there is the onstage presence of Kuini Liliha (*c.* 1802–1839), which hearkens back not only to the historical period of *The Conversion,* but to the circumstances of that play's composition as well. Kneubuhl and the other role players in the Mission Houses' Living History program "used to talk about Liliha and Boki a lot." As the most prominent historical "foes of the mission" and of Ka'ahumanu, they were some of the "naughty people" in the missionaries' opinion, and Kneubuhl herself became as fascinated by Liliha as her character Hannah was. Historical visuals also strongly influence Kneubuhl's dramatic work, and in their famous portrait by John Hayter, Boki and Liliha seem "such a striking, vibrant couple." As Kneubuhl thought about whose remains should be at issue, then, she decided that "Ok, Liliha's my favorite person; I'm going to put her in." But the dramatic—and comic—effect goes even further. By having this royal nineteenth century figure impersonate a twentieth century role player, Kneubuhl neatly reverses the whole dynamic of Living History, and in the process, gives Liliha the opportunity to explain Hawaiian history to late twentieth century tourists—and by extension, to the audience. This complex weaving of past and present is a hallmark of Kneubuhl's plays, in which any given dramatic moment may reverberate with the echoes of voices long gone. But in *Ola Nā Iwi,* the past literally meets the present in ways that theatre is uniquely suited to realize.

When the nineteenth century woman Liliha explains to the twentieth century woman Kawehi how to weave a *kāʻai,* she is also describing how Victoria Kneubuhl writes narrative. "How does it start?" asks Kawehi. "Here, at the very beginning, at the bottom of things, at the piko, at the center," Liliha replies. Like the weaver, though, when Kneubuhl brings past and present together, "the vertical strands radiate out while the horizontal thread makes a continuous spiral, turning over and under, over and under."

Deciding how best to help readers glimpse the center of Kneubuhl's work has determined the ordering of the plays in this collection. Two stories could be told. The first would be the playwright's—how she developed as one play followed another. But adopting this sequence poses a problem. Is *Emmalehua* the first play? Or given the extensive revisions made in 1996, and incorporated in the text published here, is it the most recent? Faced with this quandary, the second sequence, that of post-contact Hawaiian history, has been chosen—*The Conversion of Kaʻahumanu,* then *Emmalehua,* then *Ola Nā Iwi.* Regardless of the order, though, in Victoria Kneubuhl's dramatic world, the vertical and the horizontal strands of past and present will converge and entwine constantly.

"Carefully, carefully, the sennit net draws round to a close"—so Liliha begins what is clearly the last speech of *Ola Nā Iwi.* But the passionately desired vision of her own eternal future she goes on to describe is one that Kneubuhl wishes for all Hawaiians some day to experience, and for all her audiences to imagine and appreciate. Sitting "quietly in the darkness" of the theatre—or next to a reading lamp— we listen with Liliha for the approach of Hawai'i's past:

> I will hear the long slow sound of the conch, the steady beat of the *pahu* and then the creaking of the *mānele* swaying back and forth and back and forth. I will feel their footsteps shaking the air, and stretching out, I will see the endless, winding procession of torches, and then the faces of every loved one gone before me. And one will leave the great line and slowly come toward me, and bending over so softly she calls back, "Stop and wait, for here is one of our own, come home to us at last."

This closing vision is a Hawaiian one, movingly articulated by a Hawaiian playwright. By showing us in moments like these how the bones continue to live in Hawai'i, Victoria Nalani Kneubuhl has offered audiences, and now readers, a great gift.

AUTHOR'S NOTE: Victoria Kneubuhl's own comments on her work are drawn from a series of interviews conducted by the author in the Fall of 2000.

WORKS CITED

Burk, Juli. Personal communication re publication of Victoria Nalani Kneubuhl play collection. May 20, 1996.

Carroll, Dennis. "Hawai'i's 'Local' Theatre." *The Drama Review* 44.2 (Summer 2000): 123–52.

Gilbert, Helen. Introductory Note. *The Conversion of Ka'ahumanu*. By Victoria Nalani Kneubuhl. *Post-colonial Plays: An Anthology*. London: Routledge, 2001. 364–66.

Kneubuhl, Victoria Nalani. *The Conversion of Ka'ahumanu. But Still, Like Air, I'll Rise: New Asian-American Plays*. Ed. Velina Hasu Houston. Philadelphia: Temple UP, 1997. 179–225.

_____. *The Story of Susanna. Seventh Generation: An Anthology of Native American Plays*. Ed. Mimi D'Aponte. New York: Theatre Communications Group, 1999.

Rose, Roger G. *Reconciling the Past: Two Basketry Kā'ai and the Legendary Līloa and Lonoikamakahiki*. Bishop Museum Bulletin in Anthropology. Honolulu: Bishop Museum, 1992.

THE CONVERSION OF KA'AHUMANU

FOREWORD

The Conversion of Ka'ahumanu was first presented by Kumu Kahua Theatre at Tenney Theatre, Honolulu, on September 1, 1988. Juli Burk served as dramaturg. The production was directed by Dale Daigle, with the following cast:

Sybil Mosely Bingham	Katherine Lepani
Lucy Goodale Thurston	Jana Lindan
Ka'ahumanu	Leonelle Anderson Akana
Hannah Grimes	Kehaunani Koenig
Pali	Nark

Set Design: Joseph D. Dodd
Light Design: Dale Daigle
Costume Design: Victoria Nalani Kneubuhl

THE CAST OF CHARACTERS

Sybil Mosely Bingham	Caucasian, 30s
Lucy Goodale Thurston	Caucasian, 30s
Ka'ahumanu	Hawaiian, 40s
Hannah Grimes	Hawaiian/Caucasian, 20s
Pali	Hawaiian, 20s
Voices	Cast

THE SET

Downstage center is a free open *Playing Area*. Downstage right is a simple set to suggest the parlor of the *Mission House*. The set pieces include a table with benches and a few chairs, one of which should be a Boston rocker. Behind the *Playing Area*, on a slightly raised platform, is a lauhala mat with pillows, and a small western table. This is *Ka'ahumanu's House*. Downstage left is a lauhala mat covered with a small Chinese rug, a table behind it, and a nice chair. This is *Hannah's House*.

TIME AND PLACE

The time is the early nineteenth century. The place is Honolulu, Hawai'i.

Act I

SCENE 1

(Spot to SYBIL in the Playing Area.)

SYBIL: In 1815, I, Sybil Mosely, felt the calling of our Lord and Savior Jesus Christ. I confessed my faith before the congregation and now cling to the bosom of the church. Though I am a sinner, I now have hope that God will call me his own and receive me at his right hand.

(Spot to LUCY in the Playing Area.)

LUCY: In 1815, I, Lucy Goodale, was washed in the blood of our Lord Jesus. My family rejoiced in my pious calling. I do now truly believe and trust that Dear Redeemer who tasted death for us all.

SYBIL: In 1819, I am of low spirits. A kindred spirit to whom I was dearly attached has now departed from my life to serve God in another part of the world. I know not where my life is going or what the Lord would have me do. I feel many days of loneliness and sorrow. The joy I once felt at teaching these young girls slowly drains away, and I feel heavy with a weight I can neither understand nor overcome. I read of women who do mission work among the heathen peoples of this earth. I envy them, that they have a purpose and service to God. I pray that one day I might find such a purpose.

LUCY: In 1819, my mother died. My dear sister, Persis, was married and left our father's home. My mother, gone! Persis, gone! Wonder not when I say that I more than ever felt myself an orphan. My solitary chamber witnesses my grief as I walk from side to side. My pillow is watered with tears. I apply to the fountain of all grace and consolation for support. I devote my life to the will of the Supreme.

SYBIL: My prayers were heard! Today I go to Goshen, Connecticut to meet one who is perhaps of the same heart and mind as I. A young man about to embark on a life of mission work in the Sandwich Islands seeks a companion for this noble cause. God will guide me.

LUCY: My cousin William visited me today. He gave me information that a mission to the Sandwich Islands was to sail in four to six weeks. He dwelt upon it with interest and feeling. Imagine my surprise to hear him ask "Will you, Lucy, by becoming connected with a missionary, now an entire stranger, attach yourself to this small band of pilgrims and bring the word of the gospel to a land of darkness?" Now I feel the need of guidance! Oh, that my sister were here!

(*SYBIL and LUCY move together.*)

SYBIL: On October 11, 1819, I was joined in holy matrimony to the Reverend Hiram Bingham.

6

LUCY: On October 12, 1819, I was joined in holy matrimony to the Reverend Asa Thurston.

SYBIL: On October 23, 1819, we set sail as members of a pioneer company of missionaries to the Sandwich Islands.

LUCY: Like Rebekah, we have said, "I will go."

(*SYBIL and LUCY wave goodbye as if on a ship. The lights dim.*)

SCENE 2

(*A spot to KA'AHUMANU in the Playing Area.*)

KA'AHUMANU: Here is why I, Ka'ahumanu, Kuhina Nui *(co-ruler)* and widow of Kamehameha, have done these things. For many years now we have seen these haole, these foreign men among us. We know that they break the kapu *(taboo)* laws. Do the gods come to punish them? No! Some of the women have gone to the ships and have eaten with these haole men. Do the gods come to punish them? No! So why should it be that they will come to punish us at all? I think these beliefs are nothing, false. And here is another thing. We know where the punishment comes from. It does not come from gods. It comes from men. It comes from the priests who grow greedy for power. And who is it who hates most this kapu law of eating? We, women of the ali'i *(chiefly class)*. We do not want a lowly place any more, and the men of the priesthood will see this! You should have seen the fear in their faces when we sat to eat. Hewahewa made a great prayer to the gods. Liholiho, the king, approached the women's table. Many of the faces in the crowd became as white as the full moon. Liholiho sat with us to eat. He ate and the people waited in silence, waited for the terrible wrath of the gods . . . which never came! Then a great cry rose from the women. "'Ai noa *(free eating)*, 'ai noa! The kapu laws are ended! The gods are false."

(*Blackout.*)

SCENE 3

(*The sound of a rough sea. SYBIL enter the Playing Area.*)

SYBIL: What can I say to you my sisters this morning? I can tell you. Could your eye glance across the great water and catch this little bark ascending and descending the mountainous waves which contain your dear sister, your hands would be involuntarily extended for her relief, and your cry would be to save her. The sea runs very high, while the wind runs through the naked riggings as you may have heard it on a November's day, through the leafless trees of a majestic forest. The dashing of the waves on deck, the frequent falling of something below, the violent motion of the vessel going up and then down, would seem to conspire to terrify and distress. Yet, I feel my mind calm, as if by a winter's fire in my own land. Is this not the mercy of God?

(*LUCY moves into the light. She is somewhat nervous.*)

SYBIL: Lucy, what are you doing out here?

LUCY: I felt so sick shut up in there!

SYBIL: It's very rough.

LUCY:	How long have we been at sea?
SYBIL:	About sixty days.
LUCY:	And still not halfway there.
SYBIL:	Lucy, are you all right?
LUCY:	I'm frightened by the sea today.
SYBIL:	*(Placing her arm around her)* You are safe.
LUCY:	What do you think will really happen to us, Sybil?
SYBIL:	I don't know, Lucy.
LUCY:	*(Building)* You know anything, anything could happen to us out here in the sea, in the middle of nowhere. No one would know and no one would care. Why did I come here?
SYBIL:	God called you.
LUCY:	Suppose they don't want us in their islands? Suppose they aren't friendly? The sailors say . . .
SYBIL:	Don't listen to what the sailors say!
LUCY:	*(She sinks down)* I hate the ocean and I hate this ship!
SYBIL:	Now we must lean on Him. Give all your thoughts and all your fears to Him.
LUCY:	I'm trying.
SYBIL:	And think on the poor heathen, Lucy, whose immortal souls languish in darkness. Who will give them the Bible and tell them of the Savior if not us? Think of the Hawaiian people who will enjoy that grace because someone such as Lucy Thurston was willing to say "I will go."

(Blackout.)

SCENE 4

(*Lights to Hannah's House. HANNAH sits playing with a ribbon. PALI enters from the Playing Area.*)

PALI: Hannah, Hannah, have you heard?

HANNAH: What?

PALI: A war!

HANNAH: What are you talking about?

PALI: On Hawaiʻi.

HANNAH: Get in here and be quiet.

PALI: Why?

HANNAH: My father is drinking with some haole (*white*) men. When they get drunk, they might come looking for me.

PALI: I'm glad my father isn't a haole.

HANNAH: Hah! You don't even know who your father is.

PALI: I do so!

HANNAH: Who then, who? . . . See? You don't know.

PALI: Well, at least I'm not chased around by haole men.

HANNAH: Because you aren't as pretty as me.

PALI: No, because I'm not hapa haole (*part white*). I don't look like them.

HANNAH: They aren't so bad. It's only when they're sick with rum.

PALI: Are haole men better than a kanaka (*Hawaiian*)?

HANNAH: I never went with a kanaka. My father would beat me until I couldn't walk. Besides, now I'm Davis's woman.

PALI: Will you have another baby with him?

HANNAH: Shut up, Pali. You're nothing but a chicken, clucking gossip all over the village. Now, tell me of this battle.

PALI: No, you told me to shut up. You think I'm stupid?

HANNAH: All right, I'm sorry. Tell me.

PALI: No!

HANNAH: Come on, Pali. Look, I'll give you this pretty ribbon, see? Everyone will envy you.

PALI: What should I do with it?

HANNAH: Tie it up in your hair. See how pretty it is?

PALI: Where did you get this?

HANNAH: I have a lot of them.

PALI: You're lucky.

HANNAH: Now tell me.

PALI: It's because of the free eating and the defying of the kapu. The chief Kekuaokalani and his followers don't like the old gods going. He doesn't like the way Ka'ahumanu has begun to burn the images in the temples. He will fight with Ka'ahumanu and Liholiho.

HANNAH: My father said this would happen.

PALI: What do you think of the kapu?

HANNAH: Lies!

PALI: How do you know?

HANNAH: I know! There are no such foolish beliefs in other places. I have heard the talk of foreigners.

PALI: And there is never any punishment?

HANNAH:	No! And be quiet! I told you, I don't want them to hear us.
PALI:	Blood will be spilled.
HANNAH:	It's a foolish war. A fight over nothing.
PALI:	Everyone knows Ka'ahumanu will win.
HANNAH:	I don't care. My life won't change.

(*Lights down.*)

SCENE 5

(*Lights to Ka'ahumanu's House. KA'AHUMANU sits on her mats.*)

KA'AHUMANU: I knew our lives would change forever. I knew that when I did this thing. There was blood spilled. Turmoil rose among the people. Kekuaokalani moved his forces out of Ka'awaloa. We met them at Kuamo'o. We had guns, that is why we won. From Kamehameha, I learned to strike swiftly and with strength. But my heart weeps for the death of Kekuaokalani and his faithful woman Manono, who fought by his side. Now the old gods have lost their power, and will go. (*Pause*) Have I done right? Or have I done great evil? I took down what I knew to be false, but will I, Ka'ahumanu, be able to guide these islands, be able to guide the people? The people now have no gods, only the ali'i. How will I steer the canoe?

(*Enter PALI.*)

PALI: My ali'i.

KA'AHUMANU: Ah, Pali, my pua (*flower*). You are well?

PALI: Yes, thank you. (*Pause*) A ship has come.

KA'AHUMANU:	*(Sighs)* Many ships come. Too many.
PALI:	This one brings white men and—
KA'AHUMANU:	They all bring white men.
PALI:	And haole women! And they say they are bringing a new god!
KA'AHUMANU:	Women?
PALI:	*(Excited)* 'Ae!
KA'AHUMANU:	This is a new sight. Perhaps I will come to see them—after I go fishing. You will come fishing with me?
PALI:	Well, if it is your wish.
KA'AHUMANU:	No, I can see your mind is filled with wondering about these haole women. Go and satisfy this longing.
PALI:	Oh, thank you, thank you. I will tell you everything that I see.

(Lights down on Ka'ahumanu's House.)

SCENE 6

(Lights to SYBIL and LUCY in the Playing Area.)

SYBIL:	Lucy! Come, you can see them!
LUCY:	There are hundreds, maybe thousands of them.
SYBIL:	They look so dark. It's hard to see in this blinding light.
LUCY:	They'll be closer in a minute.
SYBIL:	How beautiful the mountains are.

13

LUCY:	My feet won't know how to walk on solid ground again.
SYBIL:	Look! Now they're closer. I see a man waving to us.
LUCY:	Where?
SYBIL:	In that canoe. Next to the woman holding coconuts.
LUCY:	Where? Oh, there! *(Pause)* Oh Sybil, those are not coconuts!
SYBIL:	No? Oh my, no.
LUCY:	Look at them!
SYBIL:	Hundreds of them—
LUCY:	All of them—
TOGETHER:	Naked!
LUCY:	*(Terribly nervous)* What shall we do?
SYBIL:	*(Also nervous)* Compose ourselves. We must compose ourselves.
LUCY:	What? They're getting closer.
SYBIL:	Now, we must try to act naturally.
LUCY:	Naturally? Yes, we must. But it's disgusting. Even the men.
SYBIL:	Well, don't look! There, I mean.
LUCY:	Where? Where shall we look?
SYBIL:	Lower your eyes and wave politely.

(LUCY and SYBIL lower their eyes and wave politely. Then LUCY speaks straight to the audience.)

LUCY:	I had never conceived in my life that I would ever see such a sight. To describe the dress and demeanor of these creatures I would have to make use of uncouth and indelicate

language. To the civilized eye their covering is revoltingly scanty to say the least. I have never felt such shame or embarrassment as when I first beheld these children of nature.

SYBIL: I saw them first as a swarming mass of dark savages, and even as I looked into their eyes I asked myself, can they be human? But the answer came to me. Yes! God made these people. They have immortal souls. Yes! They are human, and can be brought to know and love our Savior.

LUCY: Some of the women are grotesquely large.

SYBIL: Mountainous!

LUCY: Some chiefesses have western cloth wrapped about them.

SYBIL: In something which resembles a roman toga.

LUCY: But is thoroughly immodest.

TOGETHER: *(Holding hands)* Here we will begin God's work.

(LUCY and SYBIL freeze. HANNAH and PALI enter. They walk around the women as if examining objects. LUCY and SYBIL remain frozen.)

HANNAH: Look how they cover up their bodies so!

PALI: Auē! *(Oh dear!)*

HANNAH: Look at this white hand.

PALI: What puny bodies! What sickly pink skin!

HANNAH: *(Lifting up a dress)* Their legs are like sticks.

PALI: They look all pinched up in the middle.

HANNAH: And wide at the top.

PALI: Their eyes are so small.

HANNAH: They have no smiles.

PALI:	I'm sure it's because they are so thin and sickly.
HANNAH:	Maybe they would improve with bathing in the sea, and lying about in the sun. *(She takes PALI aside)* Now we have learned something. This is just why many haole men who come to these islands go so crazy over our women. It is because haole women are so revoltingly ugly. How could a man find any desire for such a creature? Auē! It must be so hard for them to get children. I pity them, poor things. I will send them some food.

(SYBIL and LUCY come to life. They approach HANNAH and PALI, offering them their hands.)

SYBIL:	Aloha.
PALI:	*(Shaking hands)* Aloha.
LUCY:	Aloha.
SYBIL:	*(To Hannah)* Aloha. *(To Pali)* Aloha.
PALI:	Aloha.
LUCY:	Aloha.
HANNAH:	Aloha.

(KA'AHUMANU enters regally, with an air of disdain. SYBIL and LUCY timidly approach her.)

SYBIL:	*(Offering her hand)* Aloha, your majesty.

(KA'AHUMANU haughtily extends her baby finger.)

LUCY:	*(Stepping back, afraid)* Aloha . . .
SYBIL:	*(Haltingly)* Your, um, majesty, we bring a message of hope.
KA'AHUMANU:	Oh?
LUCY:	Of Jesus.
SYBIL:	The one true God, the blessed Jehovah—

KA'AHUMANU:	*(Insistent)* We don't need a new god. Why do you wear so much clothes?
SYBIL:	This is the way ladies of America dress.
LUCY:	Proper ladies.
KA'AHUMANU:	*(Fingering their clothes)* I wish to try such clothes. You will make one for me.
SYBIL:	Yes, I think we could.
KA'AHUMANU:	I will send you cloth.
LUCY:	Perhaps you yourself would like to learn to sew.
KA'AHUMANU:	Sew?
SYBIL:	Yes, it is how we make clothes.
KA'AHUMANU:	No! I want you to make it for me.
LUCY:	*(Flustered)* Oh! Yes! We know, I mean, I only thought that—
KA'AHUMANU:	Why do you come to these islands? What do you want?
LUCY:	Want?
KA'AHUMANU:	Yes. Is it sandalwood? Whale oil? Your men come for women. What do you want?
SYBIL:	*(Quickly)* We don't want anything like that.
LUCY:	Oh, no.
SYBIL:	We want to bring you the good news of our Lord and Savior Jesus Christ.
KA'AHUMANU:	The news of Jesus Christ?
LUCY:	Yes.
KA'AHUMANU:	Why should I care for news of someone I don't even know?
SYBIL:	Well, he is God. The blessed son of—

KA'AHUMANU: I do not wish to hear of a god! We have finished with gods. Pau! I have destroyed many images, burned many heiau. I have forbidden the worship in the old temples. And the king has spoken these things to the people. We want no gods. The gods brought only sorrow and unhappiness to our people. We will not have that again. Let us speak of other things.

(Silence)

LUCY: Our God is different. He—

(KA'AHUMANU glares at LUCY.)

SYBIL: *(Loud whisper)* Lucy, please!

KA'AHUMANU: I want clothes which are yellow. I will send yellow cloth.

SYBIL: Yes, we will be happy to do this. You must also come so that we can measure you.

KA'AHUMANU: Measure?

LUCY: So we can cut.

KA'AHUMANU: Cut?

SYBIL: To make your clothes.

KA'AHUMANU: Yes, then I will come. *(To SYBIL)* You have a kind face, but very sad.

SYBIL: *(Shyly)* Thank you. When you come, perhaps we will talk a little more.

KA'AHUMANU: Paha *(perhaps)*.

SYBIL: So we may come to know each other's ways.

KA'AHUMANU: Paha.

(Exit the HAWAIIAN women. LUCY and SYBIL join hands.)

TOGETHER: Here we will begin God's work.

SCENE 7

(LUCY and SYBIL move into the Mission House area. They imme-diately begin to dust, sweep, and go through other actions of house-keeping as they repeat phrases in Hawaiian.)

LUCY: Aloha.

SYBIL: Aloha kakahiaka. *(Good morning.)*

LUCY: Aloha awakea. *(Good noon.)*

SYBIL: Aloha 'auinalā. *(Good afternoon.)*

LUCY: Aloha ahiahi. *(Good evening.)*

SYBIL: Pehea 'oe? *(How are you?)*

LUCY: Maika'i, pehea 'oe? *(Fine, how are you?)*

SYBIL: 'Ano māluhiluhi au. *(I'm a little tired.)*

(HANNAH and PALI enter the Playing Area. SYBIL and LUCY continue to go through the motions of housework while mumbling to themselves in Hawaiian.)

PALI: But why do you think she likes me, Han-nah?

HANNAH: I don't know.

PALI: I know she likes you because you are pretty and smart.

HANNAH: *(Laughing)* And because I know all of the gossip amongst the foreigners.

PALI: But why should she pick me?

HANNAH: I don't know. She just picks her favorites. Shall we look in at the mikanele *(mission-aries)*?

PALI: Yes.

(HANNAH and PALI look in at the mission women. SYBIL is dusting while LUCY sews.)

PALI: Look at them. They're always busy.

HANNAH: Till their faces make water.

PALI: Why do they do that?

HANNAH: It's their way. *(She calls out)* Aloha ē, Mrs. Bingham, Mrs. Thurston.

(SYBIL and LUCY stop. They come to meet HANNAH and PALI.)

SYBIL: Good day, Hannah.

HANNAH: Good day.

SYBIL: Where are you going?

HANNAH: To the house of Ka'ahumanu. *(To LUCY)* Are you making a sail?

LUCY: A sail?

HANNAH: Yes, like the sailors, with a needle, in and out.

LUCY: Why no, this is how we sew. How we make dresses.

HANNAH: *(Excited)* Are you making a dress? I would like to have a dress!

SYBIL: No, Hannah, she's just fixing a tear in her apron.

HANNAH: You tore your beautiful clothes? How?

LUCY: A fight in the village this morning.

PALI: You got into a fight?!

SYBIL: Oh, no! She was helping someone.

LUCY: A man was being beaten for no reason that I could see.

HANNAH: There is always fighting in the village.

LUCY: This man had funny marks on his forehead and around his eyes.

PALI:	A kauā *(outcast)*. That's why he was beaten.
HANNAH:	We despise them. That is why they are marked.
SYBIL:	Why?
HANNAH:	I don't know. They're not allowed to live among us. In the old days, they sometimes served as a sacrifice at the heiau. They are filthy people.
LUCY:	They don't look any different.
PALI:	That is why they are marked. So people may know them.
SYBIL:	I don't understand why—
HANNAH:	I don't know why. They are just no better than animals. There are many who try to pretend they don't belong to the kauā. Some of them try to give away their babies to others so the children will grow up unrecognized. I knew a girl who had a baby by a kauā once. If that happened to me, I would kill it!
SYBIL:	*(Turning away)* How disgusting.
HANNAH:	They are disgusting.
PALI:	That is how their blood is hated.
SYBIL:	I don't want to hear this talk.
LUCY:	Please, you must go now. We have work to do.

(SYBIL is obviously disturbed. HANNAH and PALI turn to leave. PALI turns back to talk to LUCY.)

PALI:	This man, he was old?
LUCY:	Somewhat, he had a limp.
PALI:	A bad leg? *(LUCY nods)* Was he killed?

LUCY:	No, he managed to get away.
PALI:	*(With sympathy)* Ah!
LUCY:	Do you—
HANNAH:	Come on, Pali!
PALI:	*(Leaves fast)* Aloha!

SCENE 8

(PALI runs to meet HANNAH at Ka'ahumanu's House. KA'AHU-MANU signals them to come.)

HANNAH:	Aloha ē, Kuhina Nui.
KA'AHUMANU:	'Ae, aloha nō. You have brought Pali, I see.
HANNAH:	Yes.
KA'AHUMANU:	Come Pali, my pua, you comb my hair.
PALI:	Yes.
KA'AHUMANU:	You have been well?
PALI:	Yes, thank you.
HANNAH:	We stopped in to look at the mikanele.
KA'AHUMANU:	What were they doing?
HANNAH:	Running around taking off dirt.
KA'AHUMANU:	They always do that!
HANNAH:	I don't know why they won't get someone else to do the work for them.
PALI:	Perhaps it is kapu in America.
HANNAH:	No, it isn't.
PALI:	How do you know, Hannah?

22

HANNAH:	Because Davis told me! *(More slowly)* Once, a long time ago.
KA'AHUMANU:	What was his sickness?
HANNAH:	I don't know. My father said he died of too much rum.
PALI:	You must be lonely for him.
KA'AHUMANU:	You have a kind heart, Pali.
HANNAH:	He was never mean to me, but he was too old. He always smelled like rum. It was my father who made me go with him for a mate. He was as old as my father.
PALI:	That is not what I would like.
KA'AHUMANU:	*(Slyly)* Well, I hear other eyes are turned your way, Hannah Grimes.
PALI:	Who, Hannah? Tell me who!
KA'AHUMANU:	A younger man whose body speaks for itself when Hannah is near.
PALI:	Who is it, Hannah?
KA'AHUMANU:	It will be good for you to go with a younger man, Hannah. The canoe will fit the hālau. *(They laugh)* I prefer one who is close to me in years.
HANNAH:	I like the way he touches me, and he does not smell of rum. He likes to laugh.
KA'AHUMANU:	Jones is better to look at than Davis.
PALI:	Is it Jones? The haole, the American consul?
HANNAH:	Yes, you clucking hen!
PALI:	Many women desire him.
KA'AHUMANU:	But it is Hannah he desires.

(The Hawaiian women begin to play cards as they speak. LUCY and SYBIL enter with a basket. They see the women engaged in a

card game, and sit nearby on a bench staring forward. KAʻAHU-MANU acknowledges them by a nod of her head, but makes no move to speak to them.)

KAʻAHUMANU: When will you find a man for such pleasure, Pali?

PALI: I don't want one now. Maybe later.

HANNAH: *(Sassy)* Maybe you've never been with a man.

PALI: Maybe.

HANNAH: Why?

PALI: Because I didn't find one I wanted.

HANNAH: Or one who wanted you!

KAʻAHUMANU: Pali has her own wisdom, Hannah. It is not good to be with a man you don't want. *(To PALI)* Go and tell the mikanele they may join us in cards.

PALI: *(Going to LUCY and SYBIL)* Kaʻahumanu says you may join our game if you wish.

SYBIL: I'm sorry, we can't play.

PALI: Well, I will show you. I'm very good. I won a Spanish dollar from a sailor this morning.

LUCY: American ladies do not play cards.

PALI: You must wait then. *(Returns to Kaʻahumanu's House)*

KAʻAHUMANU: Well?

PALI: They said American ladies may not play cards.

KAʻAHUMANU: Aloha ʻino! *(Too bad!)*

HANNAH: No wonder they never look happy. What is the pleasure in their lives?

PALI: Many people say the men of the mikanele brought these women only to be cooks and cabin boys to them.

KA'AHUMANU: They should learn to throw off their terrible kapu as we did.

(*Lights dim on the card game. LUCY is uncomfortable.*)

LUCY: Sybil?

SYBIL: Yes?

LUCY: I . . . I want to tell you something.

SYBIL: Tell me what?

LUCY: I feel something. I mean, I found something.

SYBIL: What is it, Lucy?

LUCY: It's, it's, well in my—

SYBIL: Yes? . . . Lucy?

LUCY: Nothing, it's nothing. I'm so silly. I'm sorry.

SYBIL: Are you sure?

LUCY: (*Irritated*) Aren't they finished yet?

SYBIL: Not yet.

LUCY: Well, this is very rude!

SYBIL: It's only rude to us who think it rude to keep people waiting.

LUCY: It *is* rude to keep people waiting!

SYBIL: She is used to doing as she pleases.

LUCY: It's her heathen manners.

(*PALI is out of the game. She rises and goes to LUCY and SYBIL.*)

PALI: They are almost finished. Then you will be called.

SYBIL: Thank you.

(*PALI remains and begins to look over LUCY'S clothing and bonnet. She picks and pulls at LUCY'S clothing, not maliciously, but solely out of curiosity. LUCY becomes increasingly irritated. PALI looks at her sympathetically and begins to massage LUCY'S shoulders.*)

KA'AHUMANU and HANNAH watch PALI and LUCY. LUCY violently pushes PALI away.)

LUCY:	DON'T TOUCH ME!! TAKE YOUR FILTHY HEATHEN HANDS OFF ME!!
SYBIL:	Sister Thurston!

(Stunned and frightened, PALI runs away. KA'AHUMANU strides over.)

KA'AHUMANU:	Why did you do that?
SYBIL:	She was frightened. Please forgive her.
LUCY:	I, I'm sorry. I just forgot myself.
HANNAH:	*(Standing)* Pali is a favorite.
LUCY:	I'm very sorry.
KA'AHUMANU:	*(Sternly, moving to mat)* Come over here now.
SYBIL:	Sister Thurston and I have brought something to show you.
KA'AHUMANU:	Yes?
SYBIL:	*(Taking out writing supplies)* It is writing.
LUCY:	*(Taking out a book)* And reading.
KA'AHUMANU:	It is the palapala *(reading and writing)* that haole men know?
HANNAH:	You know these things?
LUCY:	Yes, we do.
SYBIL:	In America, many women know these things. We want to teach them to you.
HANNAH:	*(Excited)* And me? You will show me?
SYBIL:	Why yes, Hannah, if you would like to learn.
KA'AHUMANU:	Show me.

SYBIL:	*(Writing)* We will start with your name. Ka'ahumanu. And yours, Hannah. *(She gives them the pens and paper)* Now try to copy every mark.
KA'AHUMANU:	Help me.
SYBIL:	*(Guides her hand)* There, that is your name.
KA'AHUMANU:	Again.
LUCY:	Hannah, that is very quick of you.
KA'AHUMANU:	*(Looking at HANNAH'S)* Hers is better. Guide my hand again.
SYBIL:	K A A H U M A N U.
KA'AHUMANU:	Hannah, put away the cards, we will do this now.
SYBIL:	Perhaps I could come back tomorrow and begin a lesson.
KA'AHUMANU:	Not tomorrow. NOW!

(SYBIL and LUCY give each other a frightened look as lights fade to black. Lights to Hannah in the Playing Area.)

HANNAH:	Many times I have watched the ships sail in and out of the port of Honolulu, and many times the question came to my mind. Who made this great world? Why are people different? Why are there different ways of talking? What does the world look like away from here, far away? These women of the mikanele are the first women of my father's people I have ever seen. They are very different. They work all the time and do not seem to care very much for play or laughter. But there is a way they do things which I like. There is a place for everything in their houses, and it is clean and quiet. There is a fresh feeling. It is a feeling of peace, without the yelling of drunken men and the smell of

rum. There is a gentle kindness about Mrs. Bingham. And they know how to read and write! To know the palapala is to know many things. Their talk is of a kind god, Jesus. A god to whom women may speak and a god who will let us in his temple.

(*Fadeout.*)

SCENE 9

(*Lights to the Mission House. LUCY sits sewing. SYBIL enters from the Playing Area with a basket.*)

LUCY: Will this heat ever stop?

SYBIL: The eternal summer?

LUCY: It's so oppressive.

SYBIL: I wish it would rain.

LUCY: Yes. (*Pause*) Some women came while you were gone.

SYBIL: Did they come in?

LUCY: No, I wouldn't let them.

SYBIL: Why not?

LUCY: They were sick.

SYBIL: Did you tell the doctor?

LUCY: I told them that the doctor couldn't help them.

SYBIL: Lucy, why?

LUCY: Because he couldn't. It was the venereal distemper.

SYBIL: I see.

LUCY:	They had sores. Open running sores.
SYBIL:	I'm sorry I wasn't here.
LUCY:	One was in a great deal of pain, I could tell.
SYBIL:	We see more of them every day.
LUCY:	She cried to me, Sybil. Begged me for a medicine to make her well. I told her to go away, there is no medicine. Sometimes I feel as though I couldn't stand to see another face like that—as if I won't be able to stand to see another face in pain.
SYBIL:	This is the gift of men who call themselves Christians and have no knowledge of what that word truly means. Men come to these islands for pleasure without the love of Christ in their hearts. They are killing them, Lucy. For their own pleasure and their own lust, they are killing these people. They thought Cook was a god? Perhaps he was their angel of death.
LUCY:	Perhaps God is punishing these people for their sins of idolatry.
SYBIL:	*(Bowing her head)* We are all sinners, sister.
LUCY:	Yes.
SYBIL:	It is our job to bring the word of light.
LUCY:	Yes.
SYBIL:	And to minister to the needs of these people. But how will we, with so few doctors among us, ever be able to stay the hand of death which every day tightens its grip on the people?

(*KA'AHUMANU approaches.*)

LUCY:	Aloha, your majesty.
KA'AHUMANU:	Aloha.

LUCY:	Come in and be seated.
SYBIL:	How are you today?
KA'AHUMANU:	I am well.
LUCY:	Shall we begin the lesson?
KA'AHUMANU:	Yes, let's read.
SYBIL:	I must ask you . . .
KA'AHUMANU:	Yes?
SYBIL:	*(Uncomfortable)* This sickness that so many women have from the sailors—
KA'AHUMANU:	You don't have this in America?
LUCY:	Yes, but . . .
SYBIL:	*(Boldly)* Yes . . . But, well, there are good women and there are bad women and the good women do not do the things which cause this sickness.
KA'AHUMANU:	No?
LUCY:	NO!
KA'AHUMANU:	Then how is it that they get children?
SYBIL:	By getting married!
KA'AHUMANU:	*(Amused)* Binamuwahine *(Mrs. Bingham)*, that is not what gives you a child.
LUCY:	What we mean is—
SYBIL:	We think something should be done.
LUCY:	To stop these women.
SYBIL:	They spread the disease.
KA'AHUMANU:	It is haole men who brought this here.
SYBIL:	Yes, but these women who go to the ships, they. . . . Well, they make it worse.
KA'AHUMANU:	*(Considering)* Perhaps I should make them

kapu. All women and men who have this sickness may only go with each other.

LUCY: I don't think—

KA'AHUMANU: We can mark each person who has the sickness.

SYBIL: Perhaps it would be better to forbid people to do . . . what they do.

LUCY: If they are not married.

KA'AHUMANU: Why?

SYBIL: Because it is a sin.

KA'AHUMANU: You don't like it?

LUCY: Certainly not!

SYBIL: It's only for those who are married.

LUCY: Only so they may have children.

KA'AHUMANU: (*Amazed*) You don't do it for the great pleasure of it?

TOGETHER: NO!

KA'AHUMANU: Auē! You poor ladies! What do you have to make you happy?

SYBIL: We think it is wrong to do without a Christian marriage.

KA'AHUMANU: Why do you think this?

LUCY: God has said it in his Holy Commandments.

KA'AHUMANU: Oh, him!

SYBIL: (*Defensive*) If your people followed this commandment, the sickness would not spread. God is the only refuge, the only safe harbor.

KA'AHUMANU: These laws you speak of, I will think on them. Perhaps it is a good thing, as the palapala is a good thing. But I will have no more gods! There will be no more priests to make me a slave to their power. I have spoken. We will have the lesson now.

SYBIL: *(After a pause)* Very well, let us read.

KA'AHUMANU: I will read this that I like. "Where unto shall we liken the kingdom of God? It is like a grain of mustard seed, which, when it is sown in the earth is less than all the seeds that be in the earth. But when it is sown, it groweth up, and becometh greater than all the herbs, and shooteth out great branches so that all the fowls of the air may lodge under the shadow of it."

SCENE 10

(Enter HANNAH, distressed.)

HANNAH: *(Going to SYBIL)* Please, you will help me?

SYBIL: Hannah, what is it?

HANNAH: I just put Charlotte in your cellar.

LUCY: Why should you put your sister in the cellar?

SYBIL: Why does she need to hide?

HANNAH: He sold her. My son of a bitch father got drunk again and sold her to Captain Willis of a whaling ship because he got drunk and lost at cards. He said he couldn't pay right away, but Willis just smiled back. "Sure you can," he says. "Give me Charlotte. I'll take her up north and bring her back when the ship has a belly full of oil. I'll take good care of her, just for me, no one else." My father just looked at him and laughed. He called Charlotte and told her that she must now go with this stranger for many months at sea. *(Pause)* Charlotte is such a good girl, Mrs. Bingham. "Hannah," she said, "Hannah, what will he do with me?" She is only thirteen.

KA'AHUMANU: The son of a bitch bastard.

HANNAH: I hate this way of being treated. I am sick of it. It is like we're nothing but hogs in the yard to sell. What can I do?

SYBIL: She's safe here, Hannah. There should be laws so that such things are forbidden.

LUCY: Yes, laws to protect women and children!

SYBIL: Hannah, if this trouble comes to you or your sisters again, you must come here. Reverend Bingham will stand up for you or any other woman who is forced to such a thing.

LUCY: And so will Reverend Thurston, Hannah.

SYBIL: Perhaps we should pray for your father, Hannah.

HANNAH: HIM!?

SYBIL: He needs your prayers.

LUCY: His heart is dark.

HANNAH: *(Emotion)* He is no good.

SYBIL: That is why he needs your prayers.

HANNAH: *(Obedient)* Yes.

SYBIL: *(To KA'AHUMANU)* Will you join our prayers?

(KA'AHUMANU shakes her head, no.)

SYBIL: Hannah, please lead us in prayer.

HANNAH: Me?

SYBIL:	'Ae.
HANNAH:	Please, Jesus, come to my father's sick heart. Make him well again. Make him see the bad things he does to me and my sisters, how he hurts us and makes us suffer. Make him turn away from the evil things he does so his soul will be saved from the place of fires. We ask these things in Jesus' name, Amene.
KA'AHUMANU:	*(To SYBIL)* Why do you wish good things for a bad man?
SYBIL:	It is the Christian way.
KA'AHUMANU:	Why?
SYBIL:	We feel that it is those who do bad things that most need our prayers. That with the help of God they might change their ways.

(*Pause.*)

KA'AHUMANU:	Perhaps I will hear more of these laws of which you speak. You will advise me.
SYBIL:	On this matter, you must speak to Reverend Bingham.
KA'AHUMANU:	Why? You have a wisdom I like better.
LUCY:	We are not suited to advise you about laws.
KA'AHUMANU:	But you told me about them.
LUCY:	Yes, but we can't advise you. That would be politics.
SYBIL:	You see, as ladies it is not a part of our sphere.
LUCY:	The home is our world.
SYBIL:	We must not make laws.
KA'AHUMANU:	You will not make laws, but you will obey them?

SYBIL: We will.

KA'AHUMANU: I feel as if I'm walking through a forest of hau. Come Hannah, I wish to go. Your sister will be safe here. If anyone goes near her, they'll face my anger. Aloha.

LUCY: Aloha.

SYBIL: Aloha nō.

(*KA'AHUMANU and HANNAH move to the Playing Area.*)

SCENE 11

KA'AHUMANU: What do you think of these things, Hannah? Laws, and a marriage to only one man.

HANNAH: It would be good if there was a law that would keep Charlotte safe.

KA'AHUMANU: Or a marriage that would have kept Jones from leaving you?

HANNAH: You know?

KA'AHUMANU: 'Ae.

HANNAH: I suppose the whole village knows.

KA'AHUMANU: It's likely. He's gone for good?

HANNAH: Do we ever know if they're gone for good?

KA'AHUMANU: He went to America?

HANNAH: If I had been his Christian wife, he would have taken me.

KA'AHUMANU: You would wish to be as the haole women with a man?

HANNAH: Perhaps.

KA'AHUMANU: Their god is a man, and their men are gods.

HANNAH:	Perhaps it is their love.
KA'AHUMANU:	It's easier to love a man than a god, Hannah.
HANNAH:	'A'ole maopopo ia'u. (*I don't understand.*)

(*They enter Ka'ahumanu's House and sit.*)

KA'AHUMANU:	I watched Kamehameha. I saw all the women bow down to him like a god. Do you know why he loved me? Because he knew I was powerful and did not fear him. (*She laughs*) My own father, Ke'eaumoku, told him "You have only one person to truly fear in your kingdom. Only one person to take away your rule—your own woman, Ka'ahumanu. For if she chose to rise up against you, the people love her so much, they would follow." So you see, I stood on the same mountain, looked into the same valley, and when I looked at him, I saw a man, not a god.
HANNAH:	And what did he see?
KA'AHUMANU:	(*After a pause*) That would be for him to say, Hannah.
HANNAH:	You don't like this idea of Christian marriage?
KA'AHUMANU:	I don't care about it. In the old days, if women and men desired each other, they joined. If that left, they parted.
HANNAH:	But the old days go.
KA'AHUMANU:	Yes, and tomorrow comes with more foreigners, and their ideas and their ships and their desires.
HANNAH:	Desire. Is that what rules us? I hardly know my own. But the mikanele, they have given me a new kind of desire. A longing to know the things in books and the world outside of here and the ways of God.

KA'AHUMANU:	You believe this god?
HANNAH:	Yes, because He is full of mercy.
KA'AHUMANU:	But he keeps a terrible place of fires.
HANNAH:	That's for the wicked.
KA'AHUMANU:	Who is wicked?
HANNAH:	Those who don't believe.
KA'AHUMANU:	And those who do?
HANNAH:	Life everlasting. Where everything is happiness and good.
KA'AHUMANU:	Happiness and good. Those are things we need before we die.
HANNAH:	This life is for tears and sorrow.

(*KA'AHUMANU moves into the Playing Area.*)

KA'AHUMANU: Is this what they teach her? Or is it because of her lover she is sad? Our islands are in the midst of a storm, blown every which way by the white men who come here. Laws. These ladies speak of laws, and perhaps their laws are good. The old laws—many of them were foolish and unjust. But perhaps it is good to have the laws which protect the people from harm. As in the old days, if the people see their ali'i doing good things, they will continue to love and follow us. It would be easy to take this new god and make him steer our canoe through this time, but I can't do it. (*KA'AHUMANU goes back to her House*) I can't trust this haole god.

HANNAH: I know in the days of the kapu, when our hearts were dark, we worshipped the hungry gods. The gods who must be fed with plants and animals, and most terrible, with human flesh, that they might live. Men died that the

37

gods might live. But now comes a time of light. A new god who is so full of love that he sends his son to die for men, that they might live.

(*Blackout. Lights to the Mission House with SYBIL and LUCY.*)

SCENE 12

LUCY: I don't see why you have to chide me for it!

SYBIL: I'm not chiding you, Lucy. I'm simply suggesting—

LUCY: You look down on me for it!

SYBIL: I do not, Sister Thurston.

LUCY: Perhaps you think my feelings don't become a minister's wife.

SYBIL: I would never suggest that you weren't a good wife.

LUCY: As a missionary.

SYBIL: Lucy, please. I was at fault to mention it.

LUCY: (*Cooling*) Well, I'm not like you, Mrs. Bingham. I have never been free with my natural affection.

SYBIL: I'm sure if only you would open your heart, unafraid, you would soon find room for them.

LUCY: I have tried, Sybil. I have. I have told myself that they're people, that they have immortal souls, that I ought to love them as my neighbors at home, but I can't escape the feelings that come over me when I see them in their

depravity. I can control the way I look before them, but I can't help the revulsion I feel. I can't bear to be touched by them, by those dark, dirty hands. And I hate the way I am stared at by those great dark eyes. I hate those eyes, that stare at me like some animal. I even sometimes feel sickened if there are too many of them in here.

SYBIL: Our work must be selfless, Lucy.

LUCY: It's wicked, I know, but it's true, Sybil. I would change it if I could, but these feelings are beyond my control. But I have made a promise, a promise to God. I promised Him that it would never make me falter in my work here in these islands. I can't love these people, but I will work to raise them to a state of Christian civilization. I suppose now you will think me a most unworthy person.

SYBIL: No, I will think no such thing. God gives us our trials, and we must bear them.

LUCY: *(Breaking)* I can't! No! I just don't have the strength!

SYBIL: Lucy! What's wrong?

LUCY: I don't know how to tell you. I'm so ashamed.

SYBIL: What is it, Lucy?

LUCY: I've found a hard thing, a lump in my breast.

SYBIL: *(After a pause)* Have you told Dr. Judd?

LUCY: How can I?

(Blackout. Lights to the Playing Area where HANNAH meets PALI.)

SCENE 13

PALI:	Where have you been, Hannah? In the house of the mikanele, night and day?
HANNAH:	Why don't you come too?
PALI:	I think they hate us.
HANNAH:	That's not true!
PALI:	I think it is. They're not good for us. Their teachings are false and evil. They don't allow you any of the joys you knew before. Come, Hannah, return to the way you were before. Be happy again.
HANNAH:	If they hate us, why would they come to teach us?
PALI:	I don't know, it's a trick.
HANNAH:	A trick?
PALI:	To make us miserable like them.
HANNAH:	They're not miserable.
PALI:	Soon your life will leave you, Hannah, and you'll be like them.
HANNAH:	No, Pali, they teach me to know more about life. They make new thoughts in my head which weren't there before, and now I may think of many new and wonderful things. I have knowledge and I will have more of it. Before, I was just a pretty thing that men wanted, but now I have a new world of thoughts that is kapu to everyone but myself.
PALI:	These things you learn could be lies.
HANNAH:	They're not.
PALI:	I still say that haole woman hates us!!

(*Blackout.*)

End ACT I

Act II

SCENE 1

(*SYBIL, LUCY, and HANNAH are at the Mission House. HAN-NAH now wears a dress like the mission women. SYBIL quizzes HANNAH from a book.*)

SYBIL: Now Hannah, what is sin?

HANNAH: Sin is any want of conformity to, or transgression of, the law of God.

SYBIL: What is the sin by where our first parents fell?

HANNAH: The sin by where our first parents fell was the eating of the forbidden fruit.

SYBIL: What is the misery of the estate wherein man fell?

HANNAH: This one is still hard.

SYBIL: Baptism requires study and diligence. Now try again. What is the misery of the estate wherein man fell?

HANNAH: (*Hesitant*) All mankind, by their fall, lost communion with God, are under His wrath and curse, and so made liable to all miseries in this life, to death itself, and to the pains of hell forever.

SYBIL:	Did God leave all men to perish in the estate of sin and misery?
HANNAH:	No. God, out of His mere good pleasure, has elected some to everlasting life, and will bring these chosen to an estate of salvation by Our Redeemer, the Lord Jesus Christ.

(*Enter PALI.*)

PALI:	Excuse me please.
LUCY:	Yes?
PALI:	The doctor wishes you in the village right away. There is some trouble.
LUCY:	Trouble?
PALI:	Many people have come down from the mountains where they cut the sandalwood. There is a great sickness among them.
SYBIL:	No.
PALI:	(*Holding a note*) He asked you to bring these things.
LUCY:	(*Grabs the note*) Let me have that. (*To SYBIL*) They are powders from his medical supplies.
SYBIL:	You get them, Lucy. Hannah, you will study until I return.
HANNAH:	'Ae.

(*Exit LUCY and SYBIL.*)

PALI:	What are you doing, Hannah?
HANNAH:	Learning the word of God so I may have baptism.
PALI:	Oh.
HANNAH:	What does every sin deserve? Every sin deserves God's wrath and curse, both in this life and that which is to come.

PALI:	Do you believe this, Hannah?
HANNAH:	(*Halting*) Yes, I want to be baptized.
PALI:	Why?
HANNAH:	So I can go to heaven.
PALI:	This god allows the kanaka in his heaven?
HANNAH:	Yes.
PALI:	Even women?
HANNAH:	Yes. We are all equal in God's sight.
PALI:	Then why aren't we equal on earth?
HANNAH:	Be quiet, Pali.
PALI:	How many haoles do you know who treat us like one of their own? How many of the ali'i treat commoners as they do each other?
HANNAH:	You don't know what you're talking about.
PALI:	(*Build*) No, you don't know, Hannah! Things are different for you because you're hapa haole. They treat you so, bring you into their home as a friend, because they think you are half like them. You're not like me! You've always had many more things for your comfort in life. You don't know what it is to be poor, and you don't know what it's like to be below everyone else. So don't say your stupid words to me, Hannah!
HANNAH:	(*After a pause, softly*) Pali, what is it? Why are you so angry with me? You could come here too if you wanted.
PALI:	I'm sorry, Hannah. Forgive my words. I don't mean to hurt you.

(*Exit PALI.*)

SCENE 2

(Lights to the Playing Area. LUCY sits, SYBIL stands behind her.)

LUCY: The greed of men has caused many deaths. Men come from foreign lands wanting 'iliahi, the scented sandalwood. They bring western goods and teach the chiefs to covet these things.

SYBIL: They ply them with liquor until they are drunk.

LUCY: Sell them useless things.

SYBIL: Never worth half of what they charge.

LUCY: The chiefs pay in sandalwood.

SYBIL: The maka'āinana must go to cut the wood.

LUCY: Holes the size of ships are dug.

SYBIL: The commoners must fill them with wood.

LUCY: Piculs.

SYBIL: 133 and 1/3 pounds, one picul.

LUCY: The wood grows high in the mountains.

SYBIL: Many leave their fields unattended.

LUCY: Kalo *(taro)* rots.

SYBIL: The sweet potatoes are eaten by worms.

LUCY: Men, women, mothers with their children go.

SYBIL: Today, many died.

LUCY: Tomorrow many more.

SYBIL: The people stayed too long.

LUCY: The winds blew too cold.

SYBIL: The rain came too hard.

LUCY: Not enough food.

SYBIL:	Exposed to nature's elements.
LUCY:	Not enough to keep warm.
SYBIL:	They came down from the green hills crying, for the dead they left behind.
LUCY:	All for what?
SYBIL:	So a few foreigners could increase their wealth.
LUCY:	Buy lace for their wives.
SYBIL:	Crystal for their tables.
LUCY:	Stallions for their sons.
SYBIL:	*(Coming forward)* My dear sisters, if you could only see with what misery and death the foundations of wealthy lives in America, comfortable and safe, are built on! These were once a thriving people. The white men who come here for profits from sandalwood, profits from whale oil, or for the pleasure of women, I am ashamed to call my countrymen. If you had seen what I saw today— men, women, and children dying—I'm sure you would not hesitate to lay down your beautiful silk dresses, your colored ribbons, your lace gloves and all the finery that surrounds you, to take up a Christian vow of service and poverty so that you would never again prosper by the deaths of others.

SCENE 3

(Lights to KA'AHUMANU and HANNAH at Ka'ahumanu's House.)

KA'AHUMANU:	Many chiefs have accepted this new god.

45

HANNAH:	Yes.
KAʻAHUMANU:	Kaumualiʻi wished I would believe. Also Keōpūolani.
HANNAH:	Why don't you?
KAʻAHUMANU:	Some things I like. I think it is good that with this god, women may speak to him. In the old days, only the kāhuna *(priests)* spoke to god at the heiau. And I like to see that women may teach things about this god, such as Mrs. Bingham teaches. But some things I don't like. I'm afraid that this god would have too much power. That too many things would change. There is something about the mikanele that I do not trust, something which I can't name.
HANNAH:	They have been kind teachers to us.
KAʻAHUMANU:	And they seem to care for the people.
HANNAH:	They do many things for us.
KAʻAHUMANU:	*(Bewildered)* Yes. *(Pause)* You know, Hannah, when I was younger, I felt so strong. That is the good thing about youth, to feel strong in body and purpose. I was not afraid. I saw something to do, and I did it. But everything is changed with the coming of foreigners. Their wealth, ships, guns—these things change everything. They have made the power of the chiefs weak. I make a law against the sale of rum. A ship comes full of men eager for drink. If the captain does not like the kapu, he says "Sell us rum, or we'll fire our cannon on your town!" Or perhaps he sends an angry mob to fight and make trouble. What am I to do? Keep the law and have destruction? If we engage him in battle, more and more ships with guns will come from his country. Should I relent and give

him rum, this makes the chiefs look weak. What will I do? In former days, I did not hesitate to act. My mind did not trouble me. The way was clear. I was not afraid to do away with what I knew to be false or to take up what I wished. But now . . .

HANNAH: Everything has changed so much. I know.

KA'AHUMANU: 'Ae, the chiefs pass. All the old ones, my counselors and friends. Keōpūolani, gone. My own Kaumuali'i, gone! Kalanimoku grows so old. His strength fades. Our people die. I feel as if I am surrounded by darkness.

(*The lights go very soft to a spot on KA'AHUMANU alone. She chants a kanikau, a mourning chant.*)

KA'AHUMANU: Aloha wale hoi 'oe—
O 'oe ho'i kekahi a Ka-maka-a-ola-o-Kane,
O 'olua ia Lani
Elua ia Lani nui pueo 'ula,
E Kaha'i-lani-moku, o Kaha'i-ku,
O ke ku haili lani kapu o Kane,
O ka pohaku lani ia i halulu aku nei,
I ka'a pono aku nei ma ke alo o Wakea,
E ke kama lani a Ka-lani-honua-kini,
O ku'u makuakane lani,
Hoa aloha wale ia la
He aloha ia la e
Aloha aku au a pau ke aho,
Uwe aku ho'i o ka hoa mai ke anu,
O ku'u hoa mai ka ua 'apo pu'e kahi,
'Apo mai ana ke ko'eko'e,
E ho'opuni mai ana ke anu,
A poniponi i ke anu 'a'ohe wahawaha,
Elua no wahi e mehana ai,
O ke ahi lalaku i ke hale,
O ka lua o ke ahi, o ka lua kapa,
I ka lua poli o ka hoa e mehana'i e
Eia la, aia la, eia la e—

(Love to you,
To you who were like Ka-maka-a-ola-o-kane,
For you two were chiefs,
Two great chiefs like two red owls,
Kaha'i-lani-moku, Kaha'i-ku,
The sacred tabu chiefs of Kane.
Like a peal of thunder is your tread
Reverberating to the presence of Wakea,
Here is the divine child of a multitude of
    sacred offspring,
My father and chief,
My beloved companion,
My loved one.
I am breathless with grieving for you,
I weep for my companion in the cold,
My companion of the chilly rain.
The chill encircles me,
The cold surrounds me,
Purple with cold not rejected,
Only two places to find warmth—
The bed mate at home,
    (literally, the blazing fire within the house)
The tapa covering is the second warmth,
Found in the bosom of a companion,
It is there, it is there, it is there..)

(Traditional chant composed by Ka'ahumanu.
Reprinted with permission from Ruling Chiefs
of Hawaii, *written by Samuel Mānaiakalani*
Kamakau, © *1992 by the Kamehameha*
Schools Press.)

(She lies on the mat. HANNAH covers her with a quilt, and exits.
VOICES speak from the darkness, rising to confusion and chaos.)

VOICE 1:   Why did you destroy the old ones?

VOICE 2:   Why?

VOICE 3:   Why?

VOICE 4:   Why?

VOICE 1:	Your people are dying!
VOICE 2:	Why?
VOICE 3:	Do something!
VOICE 4:	Can't you do anything?
VOICE 1:	Too many haole.
VOICE 2:	Another warship.
VOICE 3:	Another government.
VOICE 4:	Give us sandalwood.
VOICE 1:	Women. Where are the women!
VOICE 2:	And rum, more rum.
VOICE 3:	Call for a warship. These chiefs can't tell us what to do.
VOICE 4:	I'll do what I like. This isn't America.
VOICE 1:	England.
VOICE 2:	France.
VOICE 3:	These aren't civilized human beings.
VOICE 4:	Take care of your own people.
VOICE 1:	Take care!
VOICE 2:	Can't you do anything?
VOICE 3:	There's too much sickness.
VOICE 4:	I need some land.
VOICE 1:	Send for a warship. I want to be paid!
VOICE 2:	These are only native chiefs.
VOICE 3:	Stupid savages!
KA'AHUMANU:	Why is it so hot?
VOICE 4:	There aren't enough children anymore.
VOICE 1:	Why did you leave the old gods?

VOICE 2:	Can't you do something?
KA'AHUMANU:	It's too hot.
VOICE 3:	What does every sin deserve?
VOICE 4:	Everyone will die!
VOICE 1:	Die!
VOICE 2:	It's too hot!
VOICE 3:	Why can't you do anything?
VOICE 4:	Why?
ALL VOICES:	WE'RE DYING! We're all dying. Do something.

SCENE 4

(*Enter LUCY and SYBIL. They bathe KA'AHUMANU'S face with damp cloths.*)

LUCY:	Is she improved?
SYBIL:	Not much. Her fever is still very high.
LUCY:	You should rest.
SYBIL:	I'm fine. It's you I worry over.
LUCY:	You've been here all day. You could become ill yourself.
SYBIL:	I've had a little sleep.

(*PALI has softly entered.*)

PALI:	Will she die?
SYBIL:	(*Frightened*) No, she won't die!
PALI:	Put her in the stream.
SYBIL:	No Pali, it could make her much worse.

PALI:	She'll burn up inside.
LUCY:	Such a stupid belief!

(*Exit PALI, quickly.*)

SYBIL:	Sister Thurston.
LUCY:	I know, I spoke too sharply.
SYBIL:	People listen to those whom they feel to be kind-hearted.
LUCY:	It always happens when I feel tired.
SYBIL:	(*Urgently*) Perhaps you should go back to the mission and get Reverend Bingham and the doctor.
LUCY:	Is she going?
SYBIL:	I don't know. I can't tell if the fever is breaking or if she's falling into a worse state.
LUCY:	I'll hurry.

(*Exit LUCY.*)

KA'AHUMANU:	(*Mumbling*) No, no. I'm too hot. Go! Go! Go away. . . . I won't go there. . . . No . . . no . . . (*She opens her eyes slowly and looks at SYBIL*) Binamuwahine!
SYBIL:	(*Smiling*) Yes, I'm here.
KA'AHUMANU:	I'm very sick?
SYBIL:	Yes.
KA'AHUMANU:	I had a terrible dream. I saw that place.
SYBIL:	What place?
KA'AHUMANU:	The place of fires. (*She tries to sit up*)
SYBIL:	You must lie down.
KA'AHUMANU:	It was a terrible place. I saw my people burning. It was so hot. Great rivers of lava.

SYBIL:	It's all right. You're here now.
KA'AHUMANU:	You're so kind to bring me back from that place.
SYBIL:	It is the love of Jesus that has brought me here.
KA'AHUMANU:	It is Jesus who saves us from this place?
SYBIL:	He is the light of the world. It is only through Him that we are saved.
KA'AHUMANU:	Perhaps now, Binamuwahine, I will try one of these prayers to Jesus.
SYBIL:	Now?
KA'AHUMANU:	Yes, now. Hurry.
SYBIL:	Reverend Bingham will be here soon. Maybe you wish to pray with him.
KA'AHUMANU:	No, it's you I wish to share my first prayer with.
SYBIL:	*(Touched)* Very well, we will pray as Jesus taught us to pray, saying: Our Father who art in heaven.
KA'AHUMANU:	Our Father who art in heaven. . . .

(*The lights fade as they continue the Lord's prayer.*)

SCENE 5

(*Lights to HANNAH reading in her House.*)

HANNAH:	"I opened to my beloved; but my beloved had withdrawn himself, and was gone: my soul failed when he spake: I sought him, but I could not find him; I called him, but he gave me no answer. The watchmen that went

52

about the city found me, they smote me, they wounded me; the keepers of the walls took away my veil from me. I charge you, O daughters of Jerusalem, if ye find my beloved, that ye tell him, that I am sick of love."

(*Lights to the Mission House. KA'AHUMANU, SYBIL, and LUCY sit. KA'AHUMANU now wears a mu'umu'u. HANNAH enters, depressed.*)

SYBIL: Good morning, Hannah.

HANNAH: Aloha, Binamuwahine. (*To KA'AHUMANU*) Pehea 'oe, kupuna?

KA'AHUMANU: Maika'i.

SYBIL: Are you troubled, Hannah?

HANNAH: No.

SYBIL: Don't feel bad, Hannah. Reverend Bingham says you may try the examination in another month. Someday you will be baptized.

HANNAH: It's all right.

SYBIL: Let's continue our work. You may begin reading with Matthew 13.

KA'AHUMANU: (*Halting*) "And he spake many things unto them in parables, saying, Behold, a sower went forth to sow; And when he sowed, some seeds fell by the wayside, and the fowls came and devoured them up."

SYBIL: Hannah, please continue.

(*HANNAH is daydreaming.*)

SYBIL: Hannah.

HANNAH: I'm sorry.

SYBIL: Please continue.

HANNAH: I don't know the place.

SYBIL: You must pay attention, Hannah. Matthew 13, verse 5.

HANNAH: "Some fell upon stony places, where they had not much earth: and forthwith they sprung up because they had no deepness of earth. . . ."

SYBIL: What is wrong with you today, Hannah?

(*HANNAH says nothing but looks at her book unhappily.*)

KA'AHUMANU: Jones, he came back.

SYBIL: I see.

KA'AHUMANU: He wants Hannah for his wahine (*woman*).

HANNAH: I told him that I would not come to his bed unless we made a Christian marriage.

SYBIL: You are very right, Hannah. God's love and acceptance of you as one of His own requires your virtue.

HANNAH: He speaks so nicely to me. He says he loves me.

SYBIL: If he won't marry you, Hannah, it's not love, but only a bodily desire for you.

HANNAH: If only I could turn my thoughts away from him. I'm trying very hard.

SYBIL: Yes, I know, but you must learn to turn away from what is wicked, no matter how sweetly it calls you.

HANNAH: Can such kindnesses be wicked?

SYBIL: Yes, it is very clear.

KA'AHUMANU: I will read now! "And when the sun was up, they were scorched; and because they had no root, they withered away."

SYBIL: Hannah.

HANNAH: "And some fell among thorns; and the thorns sprung up and choked them. . . ."

LUCY: (*Offstage*) Sybil, please, come! Hurry!

(*SYBIL exits. LUCY and SYBIL return helping in PALI, who has been badly beaten. Her face is black and blue. Blood comes from the corner of her mouth.*)

SYBIL:	How did this happen?
HANNAH:	Pali!
KA'AHUMANU:	Who did this to you?
LUCY:	I found her outside like this. A lady came by and spat at her.
SYBIL:	Why?
LUCY:	She called her that name.
SYBIL:	What name?
LUCY:	Kauā.
SYBIL:	She's badly hurt. Lie her down on the mat.

(*PALI cries out in pain.*)

PALI:	I must go away.
SYBIL:	You're in no state to go anywhere.
LUCY:	What if those people find you again?
KA'AHUMANU:	He kauā 'oe?
PALI:	(*Defiantly*) 'Ae!
HANNAH:	Kū ka pilau (Oh, the stink)!
SYBIL:	Hannah, don't speak like that to her!
KA'AHUMANU:	But she is kauā!
SYBIL:	Stop calling her that! She's a person, just like everyone else.
PALI:	I don't care anymore. I'm tired of always being afraid that someone will find out. My father gave me to a family when I was a baby. He wanted me to grow without the shame. He's been giving this woman food, kapa, pigs, to keep me. He lived poorly so

that I might have life. It was him you saw being beaten once in the village. Last night he came to find me, to tell me that my real mother is very ill and wishes once more to see me. Others of the woman's family saw him and forced her to tell the truth. That's why you've found me this way, but I don't care any more! My father is a better man than any in the village, whether he has the marks of a kauā or not! He has given everything for me. I would rather stand by him than any other person! Even you, Ka'ahumanu!

LUCY: Be quiet now.

PALI: That woman only liked the food I brought to her table.

HANNAH: I must go.

PALI: I know you will hate me now, Hannah.

SYBIL: Hannah doesn't hate you. *(Silence)* Hannah, where is your Christian charity?

HANNAH: *(Coldly)* I will *try* not to hate you.

LUCY: Perhaps we should move her to the bed in the cellar.

SYBIL: Wait until the doctor looks at her.

KA'AHUMANU: You will keep her here?

SYBIL: Yes, we will.

KA'AHUMANU: She will be a filthy thing in your house.

LUCY: She needs our help.

(PALI cries out in pain.)

KA'AHUMANU: Come, Hannah, let's go.

(Exit KA'AHUMANU and HANNAH.)

SCENE 6

(KAʻAHUMANU and HANNAH walk to Kaʻahumanu's House.)

KAʻAHUMANU: How could she lie and deceive me?

HANNAH: She has been in my house many times.

KAʻAHUMANU: I treated her as one of my own. She should be punished for such lies.

HANNAH: Perhaps she is already.

KAʻAHUMANU: My own favorite.

(They arrive at KAʻAHUMANU'S House.)

KAʻAHUMANU: Have you seen Jones?

HANNAH: Only to talk.

KAʻAHUMANU: And what does Jones say to you?

HANNAH: That he loves me and wishes me to share his bed.

KAʻAHUMANU: You wish this?

HANNAH: Yes, but I don't go.

KAʻAHUMANU: Ah.

HANNAH: He comes every day to my house. Every day he asks me.

KAʻAHUMANU: Tell him not to come.

HANNAH: You think it's wrong?

KAʻAHUMANU: The laws of Jehovah say it's wrong.

HANNAH: *(Confused)* I tell him I can't sin, but he says I think too much about sin. He says that the mikanele worship God in a poison way. He says that God will love us no matter what we do, and if we don't harm others, we don't sin. He says he loves me better than any woman.

KA'AHUMANU:	Then why doesn't he make a marriage with you? Isn't that the way of his people?
HANNAH:	(*Defensive*) You said yourself that you thought it took more than words to keep a man.
KA'AHUMANU:	(*Peevish*) Perhaps my thoughts were wrong. (*SYBIL enters.*)
SYBIL:	I've come to ask you to have pity on Pali.
KA'AHUMANU:	She's dishonored and deceived me. I chose her for my favorite. I gave her my affection.
SYBIL:	She only tried to live a life like others.
KA'AHUMANU:	She comes from a filthy race.
SYBIL:	Why? Why do you think these people to be so terrible? Have they done great wrongs?
KA'AHUMANU:	They are what they are.
SYBIL:	Then think for a moment, your majesty, what if you were to find yourself in such a station in life.
KA'AHUMANU:	Me! I am ali'i.
SYBIL:	And what if your own father had suffered to give you a better life? Wouldn't you try to make the most of that life?
KA'AHUMANU:	(*After a pause*) Perhaps.
SYBIL:	And think if you were this person who looked to her ali'i as the one who should guide and protect you. What would you hope this ali'i would do?
KA'AHUMANU:	You think I should change the way these people are treated, is that it?
SYBIL:	(*Exhausted*) I'm not one to advise the Kuhina Nui, but I'll tell you what I know from the holy scriptures. "And now abideth faith,

hope, and love, these three, but the greatest of these is love."

(*Silence.*)

KA'AHUMANU: Let's take some tea.

SYBIL: No, I must go. I have so much work.

KA'AHUMANU: No, you will stay. You look tired. You lie down. I myself will lomilomi.

SYBIL: Thank you, but—

KA'AHUMANU: No! You have cared for me when I was sick. Now, I will care for you.

SYBIL: Well, perhaps I will try it. (*She lies down*)

HANNAH: You've never tried it?

SYBIL: No, I haven't, Hannah.

HANNAH: It's very good. Your body will relax and make itself well.

(*SYBIL lies on the mat, and KA'AHUMANU massages her.*)

KA'AHUMANU: Before you came we spoke of Jones.

SYBIL: Oh?

KA'AHUMANU: He wants Hannah to come to him.

SYBIL: Of course you won't go, Hannah.

HANNAH: (*Repeating*) Of course I won't go.

KA'AHUMANU: She thinks he loves her.

SYBIL: Christian marriage is how a man proves his love.

HANNAH: All your life you will only have one husband?

SYBIL: Yes, only if a husband dies can a woman take another husband.

KA'AHUMANU: You have only had one?

SYBIL: Yes. (*Pause*) Although once, a long time ago, I was engaged to another man.

HANNAH:	Engaged?
SYBIL:	(*Now very relaxed*) That's when a man and a woman promise that they will marry each other.
KA'AHUMANU:	A promise.
SYBIL:	Then others know they are taken.
HANNAH:	What was his name?
SYBIL:	His name?
HANNAH:	Yes.
SYBIL:	(*Smiling, relaxed*) Levi. Mr. Levi Parsons.
HANNAH:	(*To KA'AHUMANU*) What's happening?
KA'AHUMANU:	Her body and thoughts relax.
HANNAH:	He was handsome, this man Parsons?
SYBIL:	Yes, he was. Like summer.
HANNAH:	(*To KA'AHUMANU, delighted surprise*) I've never heard her talk like this before!
KA'AHUMANU:	(*Whispers back*) Auē! Her body is like a shore-line of rocks.
SYBIL:	It was summertime when I met him. So beautiful. We'd walk and walk and talk about everything.
HANNAH:	Where is he?
SYBIL:	He was so kind, and I was so lonely.
HANNAH:	Where is he?
SYBIL:	Gone.
HANNAH:	Where?
SYBIL:	To be a missionary.
HANNAH:	(*Surprised*) He is one of the mikanele?

SYBIL:	Not here. In Turkey. Far away. They said he couldn't take a wife. The man must go single.
HANNAH:	He left you.
SYBIL:	It was our duty to part.
HANNAH:	But he, but you loved him, didn't you?
SYBIL:	Summer. We were so close. Many times I've wished . . .
HANNAH:	You've wished?
SYBIL:	Yes, I have wished it so.

(*SYBIL stops abruptly. She sits up and looks around in a panic.*)

SYBIL:	I have to go!
KA'AHUMANU:	(*Trying to put her gently down*) No, Binamuwahine, you mustn't get up so fast, you are too deep.
SYBIL:	(*Jumping up, almost yelling*) I tell you, I have to go!

(*Lights down on Ka'ahumanu's House. SYBIL runs to the Mission House. She opens a drawer and snatches up a small hand mirror. She softly touches her face and lips.*)

SYBIL:	Please, remember me the way I was, not this old woman I've become.

(*HANNAH has approached. Unseen she watches SYBIL for a moment.*)

HANNAH:	Binamuwahine, are you—

(*SYBIL throws the mirror into the drawer and quickly turns on HANNAH.*)

SYBIL:	(*Intense, sternly*) You must choose, Hannah! Between a sensual pleasure of the flesh and what you know to be your Christian duty to God!
HANNAH:	Please, you've been my teacher and my friend—

SYBIL: *(Loud)* Choose!

HANNAH: NO!

(HANNAH runs from the Mission House to her own space. SYBIL moves into the Playing Area. There is a spot on each. HANNAH reads from her Bible.)

HANNAH: "I sleep, but my heart waketh: It is the voice of my beloved that knocketh, saying, Open to me, my sister, my love. . . ."

SYBIL: She came to our own bosom to be instructed. Mature and meditative, her mind seemed instinctively prepared to receive the word.

HANNAH: "I am my beloveds, and my beloved is mine: he feedeth among the lilies."

SYBIL: More intelligent, more attractive, more refined, she was our joy. The crown of our school. Rising to a new life, thoroughly instructed in a new system of morals, we even dared to believe that she loved the truth, but the test came.

HANNAH: "I am my beloved's, and his desire is toward me."

SYBIL: Official power and wealth combined turned the scale. Yet her conscience was so ill at ease. She was on the very point of resisting when she found she had not the strength.

HANNAH: "Many waters cannot quench love, neither can the floods drown it: if a man would give all the substance of his house for love. . . ."

SYBIL: Here is one of the keenest trials of a mission teacher. We plant a vineyard. When we look that it should put forth grapes, it brings wild grapes.

HANNAH: "Come my beloved, let us go forth into the field. . . ."

SYBIL: I loved her as a child of my own brother or sister.

HANNAH: "Set me as a seal upon thine heart. . . ."

TOGETHER: *(They face each other)* "O that my head were waters, and mine eyes a fountain of tears, that I might weep for the slain daughters of my people."

(Lights to KAʻAHUMANU, who looks at SYBIL.)

KAʻAHUMANU: "Faith, Hope, and Love, but the greatest of these is Love."

SCENE 7

(Spot to the playing area. Pali enters the light.)

PALI: There was, when I was younger, a woman who came to live in the hale (*house*) nearby who was with child. She was a strange woman with dark looks and knotted fingers. I knew she did not want her baby because many times I saw her gather plants to make a baby go away. But the baby wouldn't go away, and it grew inside her anyway. She had the baby in the dark, by herself, and when we went to see it, she told us to go away, that the baby was sick and would not live. *(Short pause)* One night, when there was no moon, I saw her steal out with the child all wrapped up. I followed her into the forest. She went far into the night and into the uplands where no one lives but the mountain spirits and the ghosts. I thought the baby had died, and she had come to bury it. I thought perhaps its sickness had made it unbearable to look at, and she wanted no one to see it, even in death. She stopped at a place that was quiet and hidden. I watched her place the white bundle on the ground. She began to walk very quickly back and forth, looking at the bundle. Then she would turn away and look back. Over and over again she did this until finally she turned and ran. Muttering under her breath, she ran away, and I watched her disappear like a thin ribbon into the night. And there in the forest I began to feel sorry for her. I felt sorry that she had lost her baby, and could see that she now suffered from terrible pain and grief. I thought these things as I walked away, looking through the black branches at the dark sky. I had gone some distance when I first heard it. It sounded like a small cry, so small I thought at first it was the far away cry of an owl. But it came again, louder and a little louder and louder, and I knew. She would leave her child while it still had life! The soft crying moved through me. I was sick. I ran back. Cold fear flew all around. I ran as fast as I could, toward the sound, but there was nothing there. I heard it again and ran, but nothing, and again and again I would hear and run, searching and searching and finding nothing. For what seemed liked hours, I tried, but I could not find the place. Exhausted, I sat down and wept. I cried for everything: for the baby, for myself, my father, for all those like me in the world who had been cast aside and now suffered. I do not know how long I sat there so alone and abandoned and without hope. When all of a sudden it came to me, it was as if loving hands had laid a kīhei (cloak) over my shoulders. Comfort washed over me, and I was quiet. And in the quiet, I heard the voice, the voice of a baby clear and strong, crying in the night. I stood and walked straight to it. I gathered up the small life I was meant to save. I had made a new life— not from my body, but from a thrown away life that no one wanted. I took the baby far away to a kind woman I knew would care for a child. I had given a new life. And now, that is what the mikanele have given to me: a new life from one that was unwanted, thrown away and treated like so much rubbish.

(*Crossfade to the Mission House. PALI moves into that space. She picks up the tea service and serves SYBIL and LUCY tea.*)

PALI:	I have made you some tea.
LUCY:	Thank you, Pali.
SYBIL:	You are so kind to us.
PALI:	No, it is you who have given me kindness.
SYBIL:	Do you like it here at the Mission, Pali?
PALI:	Yes. Here, I hide nothing.
SYBIL:	We have talked it over, and would like to know if you will stay and work for us?
PALI:	Stay?
LUCY:	You will have duties.
SYBIL:	We need some help very much.
LUCY:	But don't expect pay, we have no money.
SYBIL:	But we can give you food, shelter, clothing.
LUCY:	And your father may come to visit you here.
PALI:	You don't care what I am?
SYBIL:	We know what you are—kind, honest, and hardworking.
LUCY:	We do expect you to study the way of our God.

PALI: Because of your kindness, I will learn the way of God and make him mine.

SYBIL: The doctor says you have mended nicely.

PALI: 'Ae. You will let me wash the tea things?

SYBIL: Well, that's a good start, Pali.

(*Exit PALI with the tea service.*)

SYBIL: And what does the doctor say of you, sister?

LUCY: He said we must wait. He said some of these things go away by themselves.

SYBIL: But, if . . .

LUCY: If it doesn't? He will have to operate.

SYBIL: Oh. *(Pause)* It's past the time that the queen said she would call.

LUCY: I feel so tired.

SYBIL: Go and rest, Lucy.

LUCY: But the lesson.

SYBIL: I'll do it.

LUCY: I do feel strangely. I think I will take this time to rest, if you don't mind.

SYBIL: Please.

(*Exit LUCY. After a moment, KA'AHUMANU enters.*)

SYBIL: You've come for your lesson.

KA'AHUMANU: I've brought you some fish.

SYBIL: Thank you so much.

KA'AHUMANU: And some poi, fresh, as you like it.

SYBIL: You'll spoil me.

KA'AHUMANU: If good things aren't for good people, then who are they for?

SYBIL: Well, I guess, I don't know.

KA'AHUMANU: (*Sitting*) I've thought more about the church.

SYBIL: You wish to join us?

KA'AHUMANU: I have some thoughts.

SYBIL: (*After a silence*) Do you wish to share them with me?

KA'AHUMANU: I don't wish to make you feel bad.

SYBIL: Make me feel bad? I will listen if—

KA'AHUMANU: But how will you listen? With what ears will you hear and what tongue will you speak? Your own or that of the mission? I wish for *you* to listen.

SYBIL: (*Makes the connection*) I will hear your mana'o (*thoughts*).

KA'AHUMANU: There are many things which I am glad to receive from this new god. Jesus Christ, he is a kind god.

SYBIL: Yes.

KA'AHUMANU: He shows us a way of mercy. Such as the way you treat Pali.

SYBIL: Yes.

KA'AHUMANU: This is something the great gods in the temples did not teach us. And women may speak to this god, and teach about this god as you do.

SYBIL: That is one of the unusual duties of a mission wife.

KA'AHUMANU: Nevertheless, it is done.

SYBIL: Yes.

KA'AHUMANU: You do many good things for the people.

SYBIL: We want to do good.

KA'AHUMANU: But my heart still holds itself back from your god. You see, I remember the old days. The gods ruled over us in ways I did not like. So when I saw a chance, I took them down. I did away with them. But this new god, your god; I have seen what happens to those who choose him. He has a strong hold on their hearts. I know if I take this god, the people will follow.

SYBIL: As they have always followed you.

KA'AHUMANU: But I would never be able to change the beliefs of the people once this god took hold.

SYBIL: He is strength.

KA'AHUMANU: He is the god of white men.

SYBIL: Yes.

KA'AHUMANU: And it seems that the haole wish to be god over all. I will never be able to stop them here. There are too many ships, too many guns, too many diseases. If I take up this god perhaps there will be some good, some peace. Other nations will see that we believe in the same god and not think us ignorant savages. I know all the names foreigners have for us, but some will want to protect a Christian people from wrong.

SYBIL: It is a good thought.

KA'AHUMANU: We may be a dying people.

SYBIL: There is still hope that your people will revive themselves. Do not give up that hope.

KA'AHUMANU: You have shown me great kindness, but for some others of your race, I wonder. Will they ever lose their contempt and will they ever cease to feel that they must be lords over us?

SYBIL: I don't know.

KA'AHUMANU: Our ways are so different.

SYBIL: Yes.

KA'AHUMANU: Perhaps we will never be able to meet without one ruling over another. *(Pause)* We frightened the very heart of your haole world. Even as I can frighten the very heart of you, Binamuwahine.

SYBIL: Yes.

KA'AHUMANU: The big wave comes and how will I steer the canoe?

SCENE 8

(Lights to LUCY in the Playing Area.)

LUCY: The doctor informed me that the tumor was rapidly altering. It approached the surface, exhibiting a dark spot. He said that should it become an open ulcer, the whole system would be overcome with its malignancy. He advised immediate operation, warning me that my system would not tolerate any drug to deaden the pain. I agreed to proceed. That night, after everyone had retired, I walked for many hours, back and forth in the yard. Depraved, diseased, and helpless, I yield myself up entirely to the will of the Holy One. Cold daylight. The doctor now informs me all is in readiness. *(LUCY walks into the Mission House)* The chair, the white porcelain wash basins, the dozens of fresh, clean towels, the shiny medical instruments, the strings for tying my arteries, shiny needles to sew up my flesh. I sink into the chair, wishing it would swallow me away. The doctor shows me how I must hold my left arm, how to press my feet against the foot of the chair. He looks at me. "Have you made up your mind to have it cut out?" "Yes sir." "Are you ready now?" "Yes sir." My shawl is removed exhibiting my left arm. My breast and side are perfectly bare. I see the knife in the doctor's hand. "I am going to begin now." "Yes sir." Then comes a gash long and deep, first on one side of my breast and then on another. Deep sickness seizes me, deprives me of my breakfast. This is followed by extreme faintness. My sufferings are no longer local. Agony spreads through my whole system. I feel every inch of me failing. Every glimpse I have of the doctor is only his hand covered to the wrist with blood. It seems like hours that I feel my flesh cut away. I am beneath his hand, cutting, cutting out the entire breast, cutting out the glands, cutting under my arm, tying up the arteries, sewing up the wound. I know it is vanity, but I feel grateful that God has preserved what small dignity I now have. During the whole operation he has granted that I do not lose control of my voice or person. *(Long pause)* Kindly, the doctor tells me. "There is not one in a thousand who could have borne it as you have done." *(Pause)* Many dangers still lie ahead of me. I am greatly debilitated, and often see duplicates of everything my eye beholds. Now, when all is done, a hollowness falls over me.

(Lights rise a bit and SYBIL enters. PALI stands apart watching.)

LUCY: *(Reaching for SYBIL'S hand)* Sister.

SYBIL: How are you, Lucy?

LUCY: I don't know.

SYBIL: You're still weak.

LUCY:	Yes.
SYBIL:	Is there any pain?
LUCY:	Yes, and a kind of emptiness.
SYBIL:	The doctor says I must change the dressing.
LUCY:	Oh.
SYBIL:	*(Cautiously)* I hope that—
LUCY:	I know now I'll be nothing but a shame to my husband.
SYBIL:	Lucy, don't say that.
LUCY:	Everyone knows. That's the first thing that people will think of when they see me. I'll be a shame to him.
SYBIL:	Don't think such things.
LUCY:	You know it's true.
SYBIL:	You must thank God for your life.
LUCY:	*(Without conviction)* Yes, I must.
SYBIL:	Lucy, I have to change the dressing.
LUCY:	Yes.
SYBIL:	*(Nervous)* Does it look, I mean is it—
LUCY:	It's not a pretty sight. I'm sorry, Sybil.
SYBIL:	Oh.
LUCY:	There's also an odor, not pleasant.
SYBIL:	I see. Well, I must change it.
LUCY:	I'm sorry, Sybil.

(*SYBIL approaches her. She begins to undo LUCY'S dress. SYBIL is obviously in great distress over having to do the task. She several times turns away and then goes back to the work. Her anxiety builds. She becomes visibly nauseated. She struggles with the feeling, but finally turns away.*)

SYBIL:	God forgive me, Lucy.
(Silence.)	
SYBIL:	I can't do it. I can't.
LUCY:	I'm sorry.
SYBIL:	No, it's I who am sorry and ashamed.
LUCY:	Is it very hard to see?
SYBIL:	Yes, for me. I want so much to help you but—
LUCY:	It's all right, Sybil.
SYBIL:	I've tended the sick so many times, I don't understand these feelings . . .
LUCY:	You must get the doctor to do it.
SYBIL:	It frightens me.
LUCY:	It won't happen to you, Sybil.
SYBIL:	You were right. Anything could happen to us here. *(Pause)* I'm so sorry.
LUCY:	Don't say any more, please. Just get the doctor to see to it.

(EXIT SYBIL. PALI slowly comes forward. A soft spot rises in KA'AHUMANU'S House. KA'AHUMANU rises, an observer to this scene. PALI goes to LUCY.)

PALI:	I wish to do this for you, Mrs. Thurston.
LUCY:	Pali?
PALI:	Yes, I wish to help you.
LUCY:	You may feel sickened.
PALI:	No. Tell me what to do.
(Silence.)	
PALI:	*(Firmly)* You will tell me what to do, and I will do it.

LUCY:	First, you must remove the old dressings.
PALI:	Yes.
LUCY:	Then, you must wash the wound with . . . Pali?
PALI:	'Ae?
LUCY:	(*Taking her hand*) I will remember this kindness all my days.

(*Lights fade on the Mission House, then slowly rise. KA'AHU-MANU enters the Mission House. PALI is pinning up the hem of a white dress. PALI and KA'AHUMANU look at each other. SYBIL enters and sees them.*)

SYBIL:	Good morning.
KA'AHUMANU:	Ah, good morning.
SYBIL:	So you are resolved to study for baptism?
KA'AHUMANU:	Yes.
SYBIL:	Pali will be baptized this Sunday.
KA'AHUMANU:	She will?
SYBIL:	Yes, she has studied very hard.

(*Enter LUCY, arm in a sling.*)

LUCY:	The Christian path is not the easy one.
SYBIL:	But the one which brings salvation.
PALI:	I need a needle.
LUCY:	You may sit here and sew.
PALI:	Perhaps I'm not wanted.

(*Silence.*)

KA'AHUMANU:	You know these questions for the baptism, Pali?
PALI:	'Ae.
KA'AHUMANU:	Then you will sit beside me and help me.

73

PALI: (Sitting) 'Ae.

(SYBIL gives PALI a catechism, and another to KA'AHUMANU.)

SYBIL: Pali, you will begin the lesson by asking the questions.

PALI: Me? You wish me to ask the questions to—

SYBIL: Yes, you.

PALI: Here is the first question. What is sin?

KA'AHUMANU: (Reading back slowly) Sin is any want of conformity to or . . .

PALI: Or transgression of—

KA'AHUMANU: Or transgression of the law of God.

PALI: What is the sin by where our first parents fell?

KA'AHUMANU: The sin by where our first parents fell. . . . You read it first to me, Pali, my pua.

PALI: 'Ae. The sin by where our first parents fell was the eating of the forbidden fruit.

(At the reading of the questions, the lights start a slow fade to black. Lights to KA'AHUMANU and HANNAH who meet on the Playing Area. Hannah is once again dressed in a kīkepa [traditional Hawaiian garment].)

HANNAH: Aloha, nō.

KA'AHUMANU: Aloha, Hannah. I hear from the village that you've chosen to live with Jones.

HANNAH: Yes, but what will you choose, my ali'i?

KA'AHUMANU: Why did you do it, Hannah?

HANNAH: I thought this new god, this new way of being, would fill me full of happiness and purpose as I thought it did the mikanele. And for a time, it did. But the happiness went farther and farther away, something to wait for after death, and I remembered what you once said to me. That happiness was a thing we need while we are alive. Come away from them. Don't join them in their thought that everything which gives pleasure is bad. Come back to the way things were before.

KA'AHUMANU: You know things will never be as they were! The world changes before our eyes every day and we must change or be lost. Besides, we cannot go back to the way things were before. I will put aside those old ways because the people need a new way for the new world which comes to us. We will have laws. We will be Christian people.

HANNAH: This can never be my way. I will believe there is another way.

KA'AHUMANU: What way is that?

HANNAH: I don't know. I only know that I can't follow the ways of their god, although I know many of their ways to be good. It is something inside that will not be closed off, and this is what will happen to me if I listen to them.

KA'AHUMANU: Our lives take us on different journeys then, Hannah.

HANNAH: 'Ae.

KA'AHUMANU: *(Embracing HANNAH)* Aloha, my pua.

HANNAH: You will tell Mrs. Bingham something for me?

KA'AHUMANU: What is it?

HANNAH: *(Leaving)* Tell her that it is summertime!

KA'AHUMANU: *(Alone)* Aloha, my pua, and may the old gods watch over your life.

(Exit HANNAH. KA'AHUMANU moves to a single spot of light.)

KA'AHUMANU: *(Straight out)* Yes, I have listened to you, my brothers. Now hear my thoughts. The foreigners are among us. Many more will come. Beware, some will come like the hoards of caterpillars, hiding their hunger to devastate the land as we know it, until the time when all the Hawaiian people may be trodden underfoot. We have seen this greed already with the sandalwood trade. We must fight now with our quick thoughts and our grasp of foreign ways. To think too long on the ways of the past is to ignore the hungry sharks that swim among us. I do not look to the past with contempt, but seek to preserve the ways that were good, uniting them with what is good of this new world, that comes to us, *now.*

(Blackout.)

CURTAIN

EMMALEHUA

FOREWORD

This revised version of *Emmalehua* was produced by Kumu Kahua Theatre at the Merchant Street Theatre in Honolulu in March of 1996. The production was directed by Dennis Carroll, with the following cast:

Emmalehua	Venus Kapuaala
Alika	Charles Kupahu Timtim
Kaheka	Woody Fern
Adrian Clearwater	Hank MacCaslin
Maelyn	Jaye Yamada
Chorus	Kehaulani Vanderford
	Daryl Bonilla
	Iwalani Campman
	Ron Encarnacion
	Mark Allen Malalis
	Carmen Rocha

Set Design: Joseph D. Dodd
Light Design: Wayne Kischer
Costume Design: Laura Keanui

THE CAST OF CHARACTERS

Emmalehua	Hawaiian/Caucasian, 20s
Kaheka	Hawaiian, 50s
Alika	Part Hawaiian, 20s
Adrian Clearwater	Native American, 20s
Maelyn	Hawaiian/Chinese, 20s

A Chorus of three women and three men play all of the supporting roles.

THE SET

A round or oval dais sits in the center of a bare stage. The dais and floor of the stage are painted black. Props are minimal.

TIME AND PLACE

The time is 1951. The place is Honolulu, Hawai'i.

NOTE: Some of the dialogue is in Hawaiian Creole English, and reproduced accordingly.

Act I

SCENE 1

(EMMA lies dreaming under a sheet on the dais. KAHEKA and ALIKA stand in dim light, on opposite sides.)

EMMA:	*(Build)* Gramma. Gramma? Can you see? It's bright and bright. No, no turn it off. That's too dark. Fall, don't fall. Careful, be very careful. The dark water, it's coming. No, no, make it stop!
KAHEKA:	Emma. Emma?
EMMA:	I can't move.
ALIKA:	Emma!
EMMA:	The water's coming.
KAHEKA:	Emma, wake up!
EMMA:	Help me. Please help me!
ALIKA:	Wake up. Emma, where are my black socks?
EMMA:	*(Sitting up)* What?

(KAHEKA turns away and moves off.)

CHORUS:	That was the first night. The first dream. The night of the first dream.
EMMA:	*(Calling to him)* I'm coming, Alika.

(*EMMA moves to ALIKA.*)

ALIKA:	My black socks, where are they?
EMMA:	Here, right here. I put them out for you.
CHORUS:	Now it's every night, every night the same dream.
ALIKA:	I'm on a tight schedule.
EMMA:	I have something else for you.
ALIKA:	What?
EMMA:	These gold cuff links.
CHORUS:	You can't change it. Can't control it.
ALIKA:	Emma!
CHORUS:	You have no control.
EMMA:	For the youngest president of the Honolulu Association of Engineers.
ALIKA:	They're shiny.
EMMA:	Like you. Congratulations.
CHORUS:	Try, try to hide it. Hide from him. Nothing disturbs his sleep.
ALIKA:	They'd match that tiepin. That one my father gave me, remember? Have you seen it?
EMMA:	A long time ago, somewhere, in a box, with those old things, out there. I could look.
ALIKA:	Could you?
EMMA:	I'll look.
CHORUS:	In the garage, in the closet, bottom shelf.
ALIKA:	Emma, thanks.
CHORUS:	In the corner, a hole in the corner, on the bottom shelf.
EMMA:	I think I found them.

ALIKA:	Great.
CHORUS:	Stop and your hand goes back. Don't put your hands in dark places. Holes. Dark holes. You don't know, you don't know what's in there. Things, things that grab tight and hold on.

(*EMMA reaches in and finds the lei hoaka, a boar tusk necklace.*)

EMMA:	Oh my god!
ALIKA:	Did you find it?
EMMA:	I found it, and—
CHORUS:	She loved the lei, lei hoaka, the tusks of a boar, the black boar of Lono.
ALIKA:	And?
EMMA:	And I found this.
ALIKA:	Where?
EMMA:	In the closet, the corner, bottom shelf, way down there. My grandmother's.
ALIKA:	She wore that thing?
EMMA:	On certain occasions, she wore it.
CHORUS:	This is the night. The first night.

(*ALIKA takes it from her.*)

ALIKA:	It looks like a boar's tusk.
CHORUS:	(*Whispers*) Lono, Lono, Lono.
EMMA:	A black boar. Now give it to me. I'll put it away.
ALIKA:	Is this human hair?
EMMA:	Yes, now give it back.
ALIKA:	From dead people?
EMMA:	Give it back to me!

CHORUS: But now, now it happens during the day.

ALIKA: What's the big deal, Emma?

EMMA: Nothing. It was just my grandma's, that's all.
            Put on the tiepin.

ALIKA: I'm behind. Gotta run.

(*CHORUS moves EMMA back to the dais. They gather around her—overwhelming, almost suffocating her.*)

CHORUS: Now, sometimes in the day, in the afternoon,
            you feel tired. Your body feels like lead, solid
            lead. And hands are reaching out from holes,
            gaping holes in the fabric of this little world,
            folding you and folding you, pushing you
            down, and away and further and further into
            sleep, down, dark, sleep. And now the dream,
            the same dream. You're little, that little girl
            again, with the large eyes and the very small
            hands . . .

EMMA: And I'm holding Gramma's hand and I see
            the sun so bright and behind her the line, the
            line of women as far back as I can see, just
            going on forever. And then there's something
            shiny like gold on the ground. I bend to pick
            it up. And now it's all dark.

CHORUS: Now you're grown up.

EMMA: Now I'm grown up, and the path is too nar-
            row with steep cliffs, sharp masks, faces, and
            the ocean high and smashing below. I can't
            move, and the waves grow higher and high-
            er. I can't move, and my whole body, like
            lead, solid lead. And I hear something moan-
            ing, like dogs howling at night, and sudden-
            ly rushing animals, grey and black with eyes
            as big as saucers, teeth in the neck, and I'm
            swept up, running, flying like the wind, while
            below me the cliffs are spinning. The rocks

84

spin below me. I hear the smash of the wave as the cliff crumbles into the sea. And the water—

KAHEKA: Emma.

EMMA: The water—

KAHEKA: Emma, wake up!

(*CHORUS backs off.*)

EMMA: Papa?

KAHEKA: You having a bad dream, baby.

EMMA: Where did you come from?

KAHEKA: I was going home. I heard you scream like hell.

(*EMMA tries to get up.*)

EMMA: I'm so dizzy.

KAHEKA: No stand up.

EMMA: The same dream.

KAHEKA: What?

EMMA: Over and over, I'm having the same dream.

KAHEKA: You look terrible.

EMMA: And that's not all.

(*EMMA reveals the lei hoaka.*)

KAHEKA: I thought it was gone.

EMMA: I just . . . I just found it.

KAHEKA: You don't just find it. . . .

EMMA: After all this time . . .

KAHEKA: It came back.

EMMA: Stop it, Papa.

KAHEKA: You *know* what this is.

EMMA:	It's just a thing from before. Don't make a fuss.
KAHEKA:	No, no need make fuss. You screaming like hell in your sleep, I find you with *this* that carries all the mana *(spiritual power)* of—
EMMA:	I know what it is.
KAHEKA:	Listen. We live and some things just come. Things we cannot stop. It's like things choose us. Like when I met your mama—love came to us like breathing, and we never knew we had so much aloha inside us. Then death came too and touched her, came and said, "This one is mine." *(Pause)* And you, you were chosen for something too.
EMMA:	I wish I'd known her.

(EMMA fingers the lei hoaka like prayer beads. She is far away. KAHEKA takes her hand.)

KAHEKA:	Emma, honey, look, when it rains hard up mauka *(inland)*, you cannot keep the streams below from running over. *(No response)* Emma!
EMMA:	What?
CHORUS:	The streams below are spilling over.
KAHEKA:	The lei hoaka comes back.
CHORUS:	He lei nani. He lei kahiko loa. *(A pretty lei. A very ancient lei.)*
EMMA:	You! It was all you and Gramma!
KAHEKA:	It wasn't.
EMMA:	Don't deny it.
KAHEKA:	The women dreamed—
CHORUS:	Emma, Lehua, Lehua, Emma. Emmalehua.
KAHEKA:	That you were the one.

CHORUS: This is the one, the one for Laka, the goddess of the hula.

EMMA: I think you made that up.

KAHEKA: Emma!

EMMA: I have a husband and a home now. It's different.

(*KAHEKA looks away. He is sulky.*)

EMMA: This is 1951. What people like today is in Waikīkī.

KAHEKA: Doesn't matter what year it is.

EMMA: (*Being patient*) We just live in a different world now, Papa. Everything's changed.

KAHEKA: Some things don't change. You know it!

EMMA: (*Defensive*) You don't know what it was like. You were never kapu (*taboo*), isolated, alone, so sacred almost no one could touch you. What kind of life is that for a child?

CHORUS: Laka. Laka is a jealous lover.

EMMA: Like being an untouchable!

KAHEKA: But you loved Laka's altar.

CHORUS: Bring, bring the maile, the 'ie'ie, scarlet lehua and the fruit, ōhi'a 'ai. Kī, bring kī, the yellow hau and the royal 'ilima. Fresh and new, gather it up.

KAHEKA: You kept everything alive.

CHORUS: (*Caressing Emma's body*) Perfect. Perfect feet, perfect hands, face, eyes, and lips, hips swaying like the tail of the graceful mo'o (*water spirit*). Love, perfect love.

KAHEKA: Everything for weeks, all the flowers, all the ferns and vines, no water, only you.

CHORUS: Feed us. Feed us love. Feed us perfect. Feed us hula.

KAHEKA: Laka gave you hula. Hula gives life.

EMMA: My life is mine.

KAHEKA: Emma—

EMMA: Stop it! Just leave me alone!

(*EMMA moves away from KAHEKA.*)

KAHEKA: She became what they dreamed, a hollow space for the breath of Laka. Was right after she was seven. Yeah, I tell you, I never forget that day. Was misty in back the valley.

CHORUS: That day, that kind of day when the clouds moved down, low, so low, enfolding the mountains, and slowing down the air, slow, hanging air and the rain is light, so light, like love whispered in your ear.

KAHEKA: Was only us back there. Me, Tutu (*Grandma*), and Emma. Tutu had one small pig, one small black pig. Our family, we always find the black one. That pig was making all kind noise in the gunnysack, but Tutu, she start chanting to it.

(*Chorus begins a stylized chant moving toward the dais, which is now an altar.*)

KAHEKA: That voice, I tell you, I never hear no voice like that, no human voice. When she chanted the pig came quiet and more quiet. She took it out and made him lie on top the stone, one huge stone, and the pig, his eyes start to close and his breathing just get quiet and more quiet, so soft, in and out, so shallow. And when she hit the last note of the oli (*chant*), the pig just stop. He just lay still, make (*dead*), dead, just like nothing.

(*CHORUS chanting stops.*)

CHORUS: Lehua, Emma, lehua.

KAHEKA: Five years later, Gramma was going lift the kapu, but all of a sudden, she came real sick. Two weeks later, we buried her. Emma took it pretty hard. *(Pause)* Not good she never lift the kapu. That's why trouble comes to you.

EMMA: What are you talking about—trouble?

KAHEKA: You know, these dreams, those things before, you would see those things half-formed—

EMMA: A child's imagination.

KAHEKA: Hear those voices.

CHORUS: Emma, Emma, Emmalehua.

EMMA: A scared child.

CHORUS: Emmalehua is for Laka.

EMMA: Now leave me alone!

CHORUS: Without the womb, a child never grows. Without the gourd, water slips through the fingers. Without a lei, there is no encircling love. Without your body, Laka fades away.

SCENE 2

(*ALIKA stands at a podium. MALE CHORUS members stand around. Also ADRIAN CLEARWATER.*)

ALIKA: And now many of us share that same vision, a vision which will not fade. We forged it, together, on the battlefields of Europe. We forged it lying cold and afraid and ready to die for the cause of freedom. We forged it when we watched our island brothers give their lives to prove our loyalty, and now we have come back, come home, to fashion that vision into a reality. We will let go of the dark ages of Hawai'i's past, the days of feudalism, monarchy, and oligarchy, the days of rigid class distinctions, the times of the haves and the have nots. We will replace these days with new days, days of opportunity, growth, economic prosperity—and open to everyone. Our islands are a rich resource, too long handled by and for the benefit of too few. But now it is time for us, a new generation, to take those resources and mold our islands in our own image, in our new vision, a vision of progress. You might think this kind of talk too idealistic, too inflated for this occasion before the Board of Engineers. But gentlemen, who if not us—the young, educated, and energetic professionals—will seize this moment to shape our islands' destiny? We *are* a new generation, with a new style and a new breadth of view. We *will* create a new tomorrow.

(*MALE CHORUS claps, nods, shakes hands, pats each other on the back and generally congratulates each other. CLEARWATER stands apart.*)

SCENE 3

(*EMMA enters with KAHEKA, carrying bags.*)

KAHEKA: You sure you haven't seen your sister?

EMMA: I haven't seen Maelyn all day.

KAHEKA: Ah, that girl.

EMMA: I keep telling you, Papa, she'll come out of it.

KAHEKA:	Yeah, when?
EMMA:	She's just young, that's all.
KAHEKA:	She took the car this morning and never come back all day.
EMMA:	She has a good job.
KAHEKA:	She's just like her mama was.
EMMA:	No, she's not.
KAHEKA:	What's all the stuff for?
EMMA:	Alika invited some people over tonight.
KAHEKA:	Oh?

(*Enter ALIKA.*)

ALIKA:	Eh, Kaheka, you ole rascal, how come you not down the beach?
KAHEKA:	Ah, too windy today.
ALIKA:	So what? All the rich tourist ladies hiding in the hotel?
KAHEKA:	Yeah, taking hula lessons.
ALIKA:	How come you not the teacher, Kaheka?
KAHEKA:	Ah—
ALIKA:	Hey, after those haole wāhine (*white women*) see you wiggle your 'ōkole *(butt)*—three weeks, less, you'll be marching down the aisle.
KAHEKA:	Nah, married two times, nuff already.
ALIKA:	Okay, I'll let you off the hook, but come back tonight. We're having a little party.
KAHEKA:	Yeah, maybe later. If you see Maelyn, tell her bring the car home now! She never even ask.
EMMA:	I will. Thanks for helping, Papa.

(*Exit KAHEKA. EMMA and ALIKA mime putting things away. ALIKA moves to the dais.*)

ALIKA: Emma, come here.

(*EMMA turns, looks at him.*)

EMMA: People are coming over.

ALIKA: I don't care.

EMMA: We should be getting things ready.

ALIKA: I don't care.

EMMA: And I don't really feel like it.

ALIKA: I don't care.

EMMA: (*Walks to the edge of the dais*) You're very persistent, aren't you?

ALIKA: (*Pulling her down*) I don't care.

EMMA: God, Alika, what if they come and find us—

ALIKA: I don't care.

(*Lights fade.*)

SCENE 4

(*MAELYN dances a cute hapa-haole hula. EMMA is outside the group looking in. So is CLEARWATER from another space. The hula ends with hoots and applause.*)

ALIKA: (*Pulling Emma in*) Emma, come and meet these people. This is Pearl.

PEARL: Pleased to meetcha . . .

ALIKA: She kept Ricky comfortable when he had his tonsils out.

GORDON: Alika's jealous, Emma.

EMMA:	Hi, Gordon.
PEARL:	I'm a nurse.
EMMA:	I see.
RICKY:	Hey Em, you want a drink? I brought this gin. Last week, I was at the Kama'āina Club. I couldn't believe how good the gin and tonics were. The bartender said it was Tanqueray gin. It's the best.
EMMA:	No thanks, Ricky, maybe later. I didn't know you had your tonsils out.
RICKY:	Yeah, a few weeks ago.
PEARL:	He was a big baby.
ALIKA:	Emma, that's Adrian over there. Adrian Clearwater, the new engineer with our firm. Remember I told you?

(*ADRIAN takes EMMA'S hand. They look at each other with curious intensity.*)

EMMA:	Of course I remember. How are you?
CLEARWATER:	I'm very pleased to meet you.
EMMA:	So how do you like our islands?
CLEARWATER:	I like them.
EMMA:	And the job?
CLEARWATER:	Great, just great, Alika and I are working on this Kawai, na, na—
EMMA:	Kawainanea Project.
CLEARWATER:	Yeah, you know, it's a—
EMMA:	I know about the project.
CLEARWATER:	Of course you would.
EMMA:	That's one of the oldest fishponds on the island, you know.

CLEARWATER:	That's what I've heard. They're trying to see if they can build this—
EMMA:	I know, he told me.

(*SALLY'S voice breaks their conversation.*)

SALLY:	Emma, you always look so sweet. What pretty nail polish.
EMMA:	How are you, Sally?
SALLY:	Fine, just fine.
EMMA:	And how are you, Jake?
SALLY:	Oh, he's always the same, but how are you, dear?
EMMA:	I guess I'm just the same too.
SALLY:	Listen, your sister certainly does some hula. Jake's eyeballs just about rolled away.
JAKE:	Do you dance too?
EMMA:	No, not really. I, uh, lost interest.
SALLY:	You know, I think I saw a dress like Maelyn's in *Vogue*. They had a special Polynesian section this month. Did you see it?
EMMA:	I think she showed it to me. Could you excuse me?

(*EMMA moves off.*)

RICKY:	Maelyn, want a gin and tonic with Tanqueray? It's the best.
MAELYN:	Great!
ALIKA:	You must need one after that.
GORDON:	Yeah, we all do.
PEARL:	Maybe you could teach me a little hula to show the folks back home in Boston.
MAELYN:	Well, I could try.

PEARL: Geez, if they saw me doing that, they might throw me outta town. You know, gawd, when I was in Vegas last summer I saw the most fabulous Hawaiian show ever. It was at the, the . . . Gawd, I can't remember—

GORDON: The Palms Hotel and Casino?

PEARL: That's it! That's it!

GORDON: I saw that just a few months ago. It's something, isn't it?

RICKY: You know, I heard about that.

PEARL: Boy, they must have had at least fifty girls dancing the hula on stage at once. And their costumes with the feathers and the flowers. It was so colorful. It just made you want to jump on a boat and come right over here.

GORDON: Yeah, but the best is the stage effects. It starts out kinda cloudy and misty, see? Then these conga drums come in and the mist clears and—

PEARL: And there's even a kind of a story, there's this guy see, shipwrecked, this gorgeous blonde guy, and as the mist clears, there's this island girl with long dark hair just sitting there before him, like she's just been waiting all this time—

GORDON: Yeah, she sits by this twenty foot waterfall with real water! Then they change the lights and the water shimmers in different colors. And she dances, just for him.

PEARL: And there's coconut trees and bird calls and everything, just like a real jungle.

SALLY: It sounds spectacular, better than the movies.

PEARL: Oh, cause it's live, the real thing.

95

SALLY:	I'll have to get Jake to take me there. You know I read this article in *Good Housekeeping* that said couples should vacation away from home at least twice a year.
RICKY:	You should try for a job in a show like that, Mae. Sounds like a classy place. I bet they serve Tanqueray.
PEARL:	Maelyn, you'd be perfect as the island girl.
SALLY:	What you need is a nice husband, dear. How come a pretty girl like you is still single.
MAELYN:	I guess I'm waiting for someone like my brother-in-law.
SALLY:	*(Winks at Alika)* I can see why.
ALIKA:	You Indians got a dance like the hula?
CLEARWATER:	No, not like the hula.
PEARL:	Are you a real Indian?
CLEARWATER:	Last time I checked.
JAKE:	Hey, where's the feathers, Cochise?
SALLY:	Jake, be quiet, they're sensitive.
JAKE:	Sorry, I was just joking.
CLEARWATER:	It's okay.
RICKY:	I thought you were local.
PEARL:	Yeah, I'd never guess you were a redskin.
ALIKA:	*(Jumping in)* Ah, Pearl, how's the drink?
PEARL:	I'll have another. What are you having, Mae?
MAELYN:	Gin and Tonic.
PEARL:	I'll have that. It's so tropical, isn't it?
RICKY:	You'll love it—
PEARL AND MAELYN:	*(Laughing)* With Tanqueray!

SALLY:	You know I read in the *Ladies Home Journal* that two drinks a day are actually good for you. It relaxes the nervous system.
MAELYN:	Let's have some music!
ALIKA:	Coming up.

(*ALIKA turns on a radio. GORDON grabs PEARL and they start to dance. MAELYN dances with ALIKA. She whispers something in his ear and they both laugh. CLEARWATER moves outside their party. He rolls up his sleeve. His forearm is tattooed with a wolf. EMMA notices it and moves to him.*)

EMMA:	Where did you get this?
CLEARWATER:	My wolf?

(*There is a knocking sound and the party freezes. Lights go down on the party. EMMA and CLEARWATER have their own light.*)

EMMA:	The picture, the picture's in your body—
CLEARWATER:	Far away, their eyes see everything—
EMMA:	In San Francisco.
CLEARWATER:	I know he's dying. I think I'm going crazy. I just know.
EMMA:	Far away, they hear everything.
CLEARWATER:	I'm drinking.
EMMA:	His death is crawling through your flesh.
CLEARWATER:	I'm in this car, with these people. We're driving to this tattoo place.
EMMA:	It's beginning to rain, cold rain, wind—
CLEARWATER:	Whips across—
EMMA:	And windshield wipers, click clack—
CLEARWATER:	Back and forth and the ocean somewhere, loud—
EMMA:	Herds moving across the plains, in your ears. There it is.

97

CLEARWATER: The shop—

EMMA: With the sick yellow light.

CLEARWATER: The man asking what I want.

EMMA: You, trying to hold that picture in your mind of—

CLEARWATER: A Gray Wolf.

EMMA: It's all you can say now.

CLEARWATER: Gray Wolf.

EMMA: Needles perforate—

CLEARWATER: Pierce—

EMMA: Like fangs—

CLEARWATER: Tearing holes in the fabric.

EMMA: In the skin, the thin masking.

CLEARWATER: Sick, I feel like I'm—

EMMA: Going numb.

CLEARWATER: I feel like I'm—

(*Blackout. Lights up. The party resumes. A knocking sound, and EMMA and CLEARWATER resume themselves.*)

CLEARWATER: This tattoo? I got it in some crummy joint in Sausalito.

EMMA: Oh.

KAHEKA: (*Offstage*) Eh, shut up you guys. Too much noise. I going call the cops.

MAELYN: Jesus. He's drunk already.

ALIKA: Kaheka, shut up and come inside.

(*KAHEKA comes in singing and dancing a silly hula. He has a bottle in one hand.*)

MAELYN: God, get him to sit down.

(*ALIKA steers KAHEKA to sit down by PEARL.*)

KAHEKA: Oh, hello, sweetie, I'm Kaheka.

PEARL: You're drunk is more like it.

(*EMMA takes ALIKA aside.*)

EMMA: Alika, I don't feel well. Something isn't right here.

KAHEKA: (*To Pearl*) What's your name, girlie?

ALIKA: (*To Emma*) You look fine to me.

PEARL: (*To Kaheka*) Girlie?

KAHEKA: (*To Pearl*) Excuse, ah? I mean Miss.

EMMA: (*To Alika*) I have to get out of this room. Could you come with me for a minute?

PEARL: (*To Kaheka*) Pearl, my name is Pearl.

ALIKA: (*To Emma*) Emma, you're okay, just sit down for awhile.

KAHEKA: (*To Pearl*) You Gordon's kūmū (*girlfriend*)?

PEARL: (*To Kaheka*) Ku what???

EMMA: (*To Alika*) Alika, please!

GORDON: (*To Kaheka*) Not mine, Ricky's.

ALIKA: (*To Emma*) Emma, we have company.

KAHEKA: (*To Pearl*) Where you met that bum?

EMMA: (*To Alika*) I'm scared.

PEARL: (*To Kaheka*) I met him in the hospital.

ALIKA: (*To Emma*) You're being silly. I have to stay with our guests.

KAHEKA: (*To Pearl*) What, you was sick?

EMMA: (*To Alika*) I'm going outside.

RICKY: She's a nurse, Papa.

(*EMMA exits.*)

KAHEKA:	One nurse? Oh honey, I don't feel so good. I think you better look me over.
GORDON:	Ignore him, Pearl. Don't make "A," Papa.
RICKY:	(*With a deck*) Who wants to play some cards?
JAKE:	Me.
GORDON:	Five card draw.
KAHEKA:	Nah, let's play strip poker, yeah?
MAELYN:	Shut up, Papa, you're always embarrassing us.
KAHEKA:	No talk like that to me, just like your mother.
ALIKA:	Come on, Kaheka, be quiet.
MAELYN:	Shall we deal you in, Adrian?
CLEARWATER:	I'll just watch, thanks.

(*The dais becomes a poker table.*)

RICKY:	Jacks or better to open.
GORDON:	Dealer calls the game. Hey, where's Emma?
ALIKA:	Oh, she has a headache.
SALLY:	Poor thing.
MAELYN:	Be my partner, Alika.
ALIKA:	Yeah, I'll share your hand. Deal us something good.
PEARL:	Me too.
SALLY:	I feel lucky tonight.
JAKE:	(*After seeing his hand*) Oh God!
ALIKA:	(*To Maelyn*) Do you want to keep them or throw them away?
MAELYN:	Let's take a chance and throw them away.

(*Lights fade on the game, with ALIKA and MAELYN looking at each other in an intimate way. CLEARWATER moves away. KAHEKA follows him.*)

KAHEKA: Sit down boy, you making me nervous.

CLEARWATER: I've been feeling this way all day. I'm not used to the humidity. I feel like I'm going a hundred miles an hour.

KAHEKA: Here, have some of this.

CLEARWATER: (*Drinks from Kaheka's bottle*) What is this?

KAHEKA: I made it my own self.

CLEARWATER: (*Drinks again*) Maybe this will slow me down.

KAHEKA: What's your name now?

CLEARWATER: Clearwater, Adrian Clearwater.

KAHEKA: I'm Kaheka, Emma's father. Maelyn's too.

CLEARWATER: There's something about her that's so different. She doesn't seem like the others.

KAHEKA: Who? Maelyn?

CLEARWATER: She's pretty, Emma—Oh, your other daughter is pretty, too, but I—

KAHEKA: But what?

CLEARWATER: Nothing.

KAHEKA: Yeah, Emma's got a good heart, like her mother. Not like Maelyn's mama, that no good Pākē (*Chinese*) lady. She have Maelyn, cheat, gamble, run away, ah, good for nothing that one. Eh, Emma's married.

CLEARWATER: I didn't mean anything. She just reminded me of someone, someone from home.

(*CHORUS turns to look at CLEARWATER, suddenly alert to his presence.*)

CHORUS:	*(Whispers)* Someone, someone, someone, some, one.
KAHEKA:	You not from here?
CLEARWATER:	Nope, I'm Cheyenne.
CHORUS:	Who, who is it? Him, that one, he saw.
KAHEKA:	What?
CLEARWATER:	I'm American Indian.
CHORUS:	Someone, him, someone saw.
KAHEKA:	No fooling? Eh, you better watch it or you going be more drunk than me, and I'm pretty drunk. . . . You come from one reser—, reser—
CLEARWATER:	Reservation?
KAHEKA:	Yeah.
CLEARWATER:	Yep. Yourself?
KAHEKA:	Hawaiian Homes.
CLEARWATER:	Is that a reservation?
KAHEKA:	You could say so—only not so much land. You folks get plenty land yeah?
CLEARWATER:	*(Laughs)* Not as much as we used to.
KAHEKA:	Ass why hard, ah?
CLEARWATER:	*(Confused)* I beg your pardon?
KAHEKA:	Nevermind, nevermind. What we going do now? More of them than us. . . . Everykind people get more than us. You know, pretty soon, the only place you going see one real Hawaiian is in the Bishop Museum all stuff up like one bird. One exkink bird.
CLEARWATER:	Extinct. Like wolves.
KAHEKA:	Ass right.

CLEARWATER:	People don't like them. They don't fit in to the domesticated world.
KAHEKA:	Ass right. And our land, that's like our blood.
CLEARWATER:	My grandfather used to talk like that. Out on the prairie, he said the animals, the land would speak if I listened—but hell, now I'm an engineer. I make holes in the earth. Maybe I'm digging our grave, a common grave.
CHORUS:	Covered, hidden away, down deep.
KAHEKA:	No say that.
CLEARWATER:	He took me out there to see them, to listen ...
CHORUS:	Ssh, quiet, down deep, listen.
KAHEKA:	Did you?
CLEARWATER:	He showed me things. They told me things.
CHORUS:	Without the womb, the child never grows.
KAHEKA:	Like what?
CLEARWATER:	Things I can't remember, maybe.
KAHEKA:	Or you don't want to, maybe.
CHORUS:	Without the gourd, water slips through your fingers.
CLEARWATER:	I got older. I got restless. I couldn't see the use of it. We lived like beggars, in a shack, barrel water, kerosene light. We didn't even have a toilet in the house. I thought some things held us back. I had to leave. I told him . . .
KAHEKA:	What?
CLEARWATER:	We live in a different world, everything's changed.
CHORUS:	Without the lei aloha, no encircling love.
KAHEKA:	Oh.

CLEARWATER:	I broke his heart.
CHORUS:	Without your body, love fades away.
KAHEKA:	Eh, come on, no need blame yourself.
CLEARWATER:	Well, it's all fading away, almost all gone anyway, dried up and blown away. I'm drying up too. When I'm all dried up, I'll believe it was a dream, an old Indian dream.

(*EMMA enters.*)

KAHEKA:	Emma, where you been?
EMMA:	I went walking. I needed to get out.
CLEARWATER:	(*Spellbound*) We were just talking about—
CHORUS:	You, you, and you.
KAHEKA:	No listen to him. He's been drinking my special brew.
EMMA:	Shame on you, Papa. You shouldn't have given him that rotgut.
KAHEKA:	Eh, das not rotgut.
CLEARWATER:	At night on the prairie, there's a million stars.
CHORUS:	Tall grasses swaying in waves, crickets singing to the firmament.
EMMA:	(*Captivated*) Now he's seeing stars.
KAHEKA:	(*To himself*) Yeah, and he likes one best.
CLEARWATER:	They wrap around the world like a blanket of fireflies.
CHORUS:	Fire, fire, fly and fly, fire.
EMMA:	(*Snapping out of it*) See what you did to him! All this drinking, it makes me crazy. Give me that. This is going down the sink.

(*Having taken away the bottle, EMMA leaves.*)

KAHEKA:	These wāhine, they never like us guys have any fun, yeah?
CLEARWATER:	What was it we were drinking anyway?
KAHEKA:	Never mind. This granfadda, he was one watch-you-call, witch doctor?
CLEARWATER:	No, no, he talked to them. He had many conversations with wolves . . .
KAHEKA:	What else?
CLEARWATER:	*(Watching EMMA)* Who?
KAHEKA:	Your grandfadda!
CLEARWATER:	He, he talked to animals, looked at clouds. He did a lot of strange things. Who cares?
KAHEKA:	I better.

(Lights dim on CLEARWATER and KAHEKA but enough so we still see them. Lights slowly up to see ALIKA and MAELYN sculpted in their frozen pose looking at each other. EMMA moves in to look at them with CHORUS, who reassume their party poses. CLEAR-WATER watches EMMA.)

CLEARWATER:	Do you know what the red buffalo is?
KAHEKA:	No.
CLEARWATER:	It's when lightning comes down from the sky! And strikes the dried grass on the prairie, and fire rolls across everything—hot, fire, roaring, burning, everything, to the ground, everything.

(EMMA looks at ALIKA and MAELYN.)

EMMA:	No.

(EMMA looks back at CLEARWATER.)

EMMA:	No, this will never happen.

(Lights out fast on EMMA.)

KAHEKA:	Then what happens?
CLEARWATER:	*(Dejected)* Everything dies.

SCENE 5

(EMMA moves to the dais. She lies down under the sheet as the lights fade to very dark. EMMA begins to dream again. Lights rise slowly into the scene. CHORUS moves in.)

EMMA: Water, too much water, make it stop.

ALIKA: Emma, wake up.

CHORUS: Things, things grab on tight.

EMMA: I can't move. I can't. Help me, please help me.

ALIKA: Emma, for God's sake wake up.

EMMA: *(Waking up, gasping)* Oh my god, oh my god.

ALIKA: Again, you're doing it again. Come on, snap out of it.

CHORUS: Hands are reaching out.

EMMA: I'm sorry.

CHORUS: Reaching out from gaping holes.

ALIKA: What is wrong with you?

EMMA: I don't know. I keep dreaming.

CHORUS: Folding and holding you.

ALIKA: Jesus. I just hope the neighbors can't hear you.

EMMA: I'm sorry. I'll be all right.

CHORUS: Pushing you down, down and away.

ALIKA: And getting scared for no reason when we have company.

EMMA: I just didn't feel right.

CHORUS: Further and further away.

ALIKA:	You never had these problems before. I don't understand this.
EMMA:	I'll be all right!!
ALIKA:	It's all in your mind. You just have to learn to contain yourself!
CHORUS:	Down, further, folding away.

(*Blackout.*)

End ACT I

Act II

(ALIKA walks to a table and unrolls some blueprints. CLEARWA-TER joins him.)

ALIKA:	This dining room extending over the fish-pond is really going to be something.
CLEARWATER:	The soils engineer is doing core samples. We should know what's under the water there today.
ALIKA:	This is what really sold the project.
CLEARWATER:	Let's hope there's something solid to build it on.
ALIKA:	We're going to build it.
CLEARWATER:	Elegant engineering.
ALIKA:	What?
CLEARWATER:	This ancient fishpond.
ALIKA:	Some of the old folks out there were trying to stop us from doing this.
CLEARWATER:	I would too, if it were mine.
ALIKA:	You know, before the war we were really stuck in that down-on-the-farm mentality. We need change. We need to move forward.

CLEARWATER:	*(Only half joking)* Nothing like a good war to clear the air, huh?
ALIKA:	At least now, we can see better things for ourselves in the future.
CLEARWATER:	Like what?
ALIKA:	Like Hawai'i becoming a state.
CLEARWATER:	And that will be better for who?
ALIKA:	For everyone! It'll be a great equalizer. Things will be more equal.
CLEARWATER:	You're talking to someone who grew up on a reservation.
ALIKA:	We fought for America. We earned it.
CLEARWATER:	Well, I hope it works out for you.
ALIKA:	Where were you?
CLEARWATER:	Where was I?
ALIKA:	During the war.
CLEARWATER:	In the Pacific.
ALIKA:	Philippines?
CLEARWATER:	All over, in the Navy.
ALIKA:	I was in Europe.
CLEARWATER:	I don't like to think about it.
ALIKA:	I think about it. I can't say I liked it, but I really felt alive then. Everything meant something, counted, every minute was important. I was doing something. I was fighting to win.
CLEARWATER:	Danger, it forces you to really live in your body.
ALIKA:	I don't think you know what I mean.
CLEARWATER:	I know what you mean.

109

| ALIKA: | I'd like you to show me the soils report as soon as you get it. |
| CLEARWATER: | As soon as I *evaluate* it. |

SCENE 2

(*MAELYN sits at the edge of the dais and watches EMMA sleep. EMMA wakes up.*)

EMMA:	Mae, what are you—
MAELYN:	Papa locked the door last night.
EMMA:	Again?
MAELYN:	Alika let me in.
EMMA:	I see.
MAELYN:	I slept on the couch.
EMMA:	Oh.
MAELYN:	You were asleep.
EMMA:	I didn't hear you.
MAELYN:	Alika's gone to work.
EMMA:	I didn't hear him.
MAELYN:	I made him breakfast.
EMMA:	He doesn't eat in the morning.
MAELYN:	He said he was hungry.
EMMA:	Why are you watching me?
MAELYN:	I heard you talking in your sleep.
EMMA:	What did I say?
MAELYN:	You don't know?
EMMA:	No.

MAELYN:	Then it doesn't really matter.
EMMA:	Do you know?
MAELYN:	It was only a dream, right?
EMMA:	That's right.
MAELYN:	(*Brings out the lei hoaka*) When did you find this again, Emma?
EMMA:	I should have put it away.
MAELYN:	You never said you found it again.
EMMA:	I didn't think it would interest you.
MAELYN:	I could use this, when I dance.
EMMA:	Here, let me put it away.
MAELYN:	It's a family thing, Emma.
EMMA:	She gave it to *me*.
MAELYN:	But you don't even dance anymore.
EMMA:	It's not a decoration.
MAELYN:	I *know* what it is.
EMMA:	Then give it to me.

(*EMMA aggressively takes it away from MAELYN.*)

MAELYN:	Sorry, I forgot—Laka club, members only.
EMMA:	I'm sorry Mae. I didn't mean to—
MAELYN:	Gramma made a mistake. I'm the one who still dances.
EMMA:	But you— (*She stops herself*)
MAELYN:	But what?
EMMA:	Nothing.
MAELYN:	I don't know your secret dances?
EMMA:	I didn't say that.
MAELYN:	You think it.

EMMA:	I think what you dance is wonderful.
MAELYN:	You don't lie very well.
EMMA:	I'm not lying.
MAELYN:	No? Then why aren't you down in Waikīkī with the rest of us?
EMMA:	I just don't want to dance, that's all.
MAELYN:	Oh, really?

(*Pause.*)

EMMA:	I need to get dressed.

(*EMMA exits. After a moment KAHEKA enters.*)

KAHEKA:	Emma, are you—oh.
MAELYN:	Why did you lock me out last night?
KAHEKA:	Why you came home so late?
MAELYN:	Look, I need the car tonight.
KAHEKA:	I no like you use the car for fool around.
MAELYN:	I've put money into that car.
KAHEKA:	So?
MAELYN:	So don't beg me to pay next time it breaks down.
KAHEKA:	Why you no act nice?
MAELYN:	Like who?
KAHEKA:	Never mind.
MAELYN:	Like your precious Emma?
KAHEKA:	I said never mind! Look Maelyn, I just want—

(*Enter EMMA.*)

| MAELYN: | You want! You want! What you want is to treat me like shit because of what my mother did! |

(*KAHEKA is silenced.*)

EMMA:	Mae?
MAELYN:	Your mother just died, but mine ran out on him—like any woman in her right mind would.
EMMA:	(*Calmly*) Look, Mae, I'm taking Papa out. We're going out. You stay here until—
MAELYN:	I know what I'm doing, Emma.
EMMA:	Just close the door when you leave.

(*EMMA and KAHEKA exit. MAELYN takes out the lei hoaka. She fingers it as she speaks.*)

MAELYN:	She thinks I didn't know anything about it.
CHORUS:	You don't know.
MAELYN:	But I could tell when she came. I could always tell.
CHORUS:	Don't tell her.
MAELYN:	Things would change. The air filled up so thick, like that split second before the rain comes, and then the wind blew in, blowing in a space, an open space, and she would pass through for Emma.
CHORUS:	For Emma.
MAELYN:	Not for me.
CHORUS:	Only for Emma.
MAELYN:	Look through the window, but don't come in.
CHORUS:	Stay outside.
MAELYN:	Stay outside in the shadows.
CHORUS:	In the dark.
MAELYN:	It gets dark in the shadows.

(*MAELYN exits, taking the lei hoaka.*)

SCENE 3

(*CLEARWATER stands looking out. KAHEKA enters, and watches him before talking.*)

KAHEKA: Hey, Indian boy, working late?

CLEARWATER: I just picked up a report from the soils engineer. He finished late. I have to go over it and get it to Alika, but I just couldn't leave right away.

KAHEKA: Yeah, I know, too nice this place.

CLEARWATER: If you're looking for him, he hasn't been here.

KAHEKA: Who?

CLEARWATER: Alika.

KAHEKA: No, no, I just drive out this way sometimes. Stop here, you know—good place for think things over.

(*KAHEKA takes a beer out of the bag and hands it to CLEARWATER. He gets one out for himself.*)

CLEARWATER: It's a beautiful fishpond.

KAHEKA: What, you not going call it the "job site"?

CLEARWATER: Kawai—don't tell me now—Kawainanea.

KAHEKA: Pretty good, for a hao—Oh no, you not really haole, yeah?

CLEARWATER: What does it mean anyway, Kawainanea?

KAHEKA: Nanea's water. She was a famous moʻo.

CLEARWATER: What's that?

KAHEKA: Kinda like one giant lizard—they say something with shiny slick skin. You know, from before time, something old and powerful, lived in the water.

114

CLEARWATER: A mihn.

KAHEKA: Mein?

CLEARWATER: We have things like that, stories about things like that living in the water at home—old, unseen things. They talk about them that way, like giant lizards living in the rivers and lakes . . . mihn.

KAHEKA: *(After a pause)* You know, Emma and Mae-lyn's grandma, my mother, her family used to have all this, all this land from the shore all the way up, all our family's land. Some of our family still live up there, small places they have now, almost nothing, almost everything gone, lost.

CLEARWATER: Yeah, that's what happens, everything gets lost.

KAHEKA: If we not careful.

CLEARWATER: *(Pause)* What's it worth?

KAHEKA: Same price as a prairie.

CLEARWATER: The cost of living is almost too steep these days.

KAHEKA: What you said?

CLEARWATER: Nothing.

KAHEKA: You know, the old folks used to say some-times, when somebody died, "Oh, he died of a broken heart."

CLEARWATER: Really?

KAHEKA: Yeah, it's true. People would choose to give up on life because . . .

CLEARWATER: Because?

KAHEKA: Because of the pain that comes from living.

CLEARWATER: I guess it was their own business then.

KAHEKA:	I guess it was. *(Pause)* What about you? Staying here long?
CLEARWATER:	I don't know.
KAHEKA:	Could start to feel like home, if you let it.
CLEARWATER:	Life was pretty different where I came from.
KAHEKA:	Except for the moʻo living under the water.
CLEARWATER:	She hates this, doesn't she?
KAHEKA:	The moʻo?
CLEARWATER:	No, Emma. She hates this project.
KAHEKA:	How you know?
CLEARWATER:	I just know.
KAHEKA:	You pretty smart.
CLEARWATER:	*(Just realizes it)* And those people. Alika said some people didn't want this place changed. That's your family?
KAHEKA:	My mother lived up there, someone Emma really loved. She practically raised Emma out here.

(*CLEARWATER stands and looks in the pond.*)

KAHEKA:	What do you see, Indian boy?
CLEARWATER:	*(Pause)* It's so still, I can see my reflection.
KAHEKA:	Imagine that.
CLEARWATER:	*(Slightly edgy)* Yeah, well, I gotta go. I need to look at this report and get it to Alika.

(*CLEARWATER exits.*)

SCENE 4

(Crossfade as EMMA appears in a dim spot of light. KAHEKA still sits as if at the fishpond and speaks to EMMA, but doesn't look at her.)

KAHEKA: Emma, I was just sitting there, doing nothing.

EMMA: And?

KAHEKA: And the wind comes up.

(CHORUS makes the sound of the wind.)

KAHEKA: And then she came up, a woman, was like she just came up from the water.

(A CHORUS WOMAN rises as if emerging from the fishpond.)

KAHEKA: Dry and she was all dry, not one drop of water.

EMMA: Go on.

KAHEKA: And she had one bowl, wooden, shining and brown, and she walked up to me and said—

CHORUS WOMAN: Nānā 'oe iā ia. *(Look at it.)*

KAHEKA: So I went look in the water, I saw . . .

EMMA: You saw?

KAHEKA: Why, I saw you, Emma.

EMMA: *(Worried)* What does it mean, Papa?

KAHEKA: I don't know, baby.

(CHORUS WOMAN withdraws quickly as all lights fade on KAHEKA.)

SCENE 5

(*EMMA remains in a dim light.*)

EMMA: I'm sorry, Alika isn't here right now.

(*Lights reveal CLEARWATER.*)

CLEARWATER: We needed to go over this report for his meeting.

EMMA: He stops at the gym on Fridays.

CLEARWATER: He said to meet him here.

EMMA: Come in, he should be back soon.

CLEARWATER: I don't want to trouble you.

EMMA: No, come in, sit down.

CLEARWATER: Thank you.

EMMA: Would you like something to drink?

CLEARWATER: No thank you.

EMMA: So, how have you been?

CLEARWATER: Fine, just fine. . . . What is this?

EMMA: It's called pūkiawe.

CLEARWATER: I've seen it before.

EMMA: It only grows here in Hawai'i.

CLEARWATER: I don't know where. Maybe I dreamed it.

EMMA: Dreamed it?

CLEARWATER: Yeah, do you dream?

EMMA: No.

CLEARWATER: Never? Maybe you dream but you don't remember.

EMMA: Never. Are you sure I can't get you something?

CLEARWATER:	I'm sure.
EMMA:	Alika really should be—
CLEARWATER:	*(Touches the pūkiawe)* It's endemic.
EMMA:	What is endemic?
CLEARWATER:	It's a plant that came here before people and evolved to something completely unique, like no other plant in the world.
EMMA:	Grandma said that the foreign plants were eating up our beautiful forest.
CLEARWATER:	Emma, listen to me. Have you ever been somewhere and you know you weren't?
EMMA:	What?
CLEARWATER:	Thought something was happening when it couldn't have been?
EMMA:	I don't know what you're talking about.
CLEARWATER:	It was something at the party—
EMMA:	You had too much to drink.
CLEARWATER:	And dreams, I have dreams, every night the same. Water, always water.
EMMA:	Why are you telling me this?
CLEARWATER:	Why do you think I'm telling you?
EMMA:	I don't know what you want.
CLEARWATER:	I'm making you nervous.
EMMA:	I am not nervous.
CLEARWATER:	I don't mean to frighten you.
EMMA:	I am not frightened!
CLEARWATER:	It's something. I thought we had the same—something.
EMMA:	I'm sorry. I can't help you.

CLEARWATER:	Won't.
EMMA:	I *can't.*
CLEARWATER:	Sorry. I'm sorry. I won't disturb things.
EMMA:	(*After a moment, very polite*) Now, how long did you say you'd been here?
CLEARWATER:	About two months.
EMMA:	Do you like the company?
CLEARWATER:	I like it.
EMMA:	Alika likes it.
CLEARWATER:	Does he?
EMMA:	Yes.
CLEARWATER:	Have you been married long? I hope you don't mind me asking.
EMMA:	Four years.
CLEARWATER:	Long enough.
EMMA:	We're planning to have children soon.
CLEARWATER:	I see.
EMMA:	Three or four.
CLEARWATER:	I guess you know what you want.
EMMA:	Oh, I know what I want.

SCENE 6

(*ALIKA enters.*)

ALIKA:	Hey, Adrian, sorry I'm a little late.

(*EMMA hugs ALIKA.*)

ALIKA:	Take it easy, honey. Get us a beer, would you?

(*Exit EMMA.*)

ALIKA:	So you got the report?
CLEARWATER:	Right here.
ALIKA:	What's the news?
CLEARWATER:	He did three core samples about thirty feet apart.
ALIKA:	Right.
CLEARWATER:	The first two—

(*EMMA enters and gives ALIKA and CLEARWATER a beer.*)

ALIKA:	Thanks, honey.
CLEARWATER:	Thank you. The first two, he drilled down forty feet and the last ten feet were solid coral.
ALIKA:	Great.
CLEARWATER:	The third time, he went down twenty feet, hit coral for eight, and then nothing.
ALIKA:	What do you mean nothing?
CLEARWATER:	I mean the drill went right through to nothing, just water, an empty hole, and we don't know what's really under there.
ALIKA:	There must be something.
CLEARWATER:	We need more samples. Maybe we can find another spot that's solid.
ALIKA:	That means more time, more delays, more money. The other two were fine.
CLEARWATER:	Coral is not like basalt, it's not that easy to calculate its load bearing strength.
ALIKA:	Yeah, well we can't go over budget. That drilling is expensive.
CLEARWATER:	If anything went wrong, we'd all be liable. That's over budget.

121

ALIKA:	Okay, I'll tell them you want more samples.
CLEARWATER:	Fine.
ALIKA:	But if I get any flack, I'm sending them to you.
CLEARWATER:	That's fine with me. *(Looking at EMMA)* It's a beautiful place out there.
ALIKA:.	Great site. Emma, I'm starved, could you get us some chips or something?
EMMA:	Sure.

(EMMA exits.)

ALIKA:	All used to Hawai'i?
CLEARWATER:	Pretty much.
ALIKA:	You know, you should loosen up a bit.
CLEARWATER:	What?
ALIKA:	You know, get around some. You'll fit in better.
CLEARWATER:	Oh, yeah?
ALIKA:	Look, Ricky, Gordon, and me are going out later. I haven't told Emma yet. Why don't you come?
CLEARWATER:	Maybe.
ALIKA:	About seven, at the Waikīkī Lagoon. Pearl and Maelyn will be there. They're bringing some of their girlfriends.
CLEARWATER:	Sounds interesting.
ALIKA:	It always is.
CLEARWATER:	Maybe I'll be there.

(EMMA enters with a bowl of chips.)

CLEARWATER:	Well, thanks for the beer. I have to get going. Goodbye, Emma. I hope I wasn't any trouble to you.

EMMA: No trouble at all.

(*Exit CLEARWATER.*)

SCENE 7

(*The scene builds.*)

ALIKA: He seemed uncomfortable.

EMMA: Why do you say that?

ALIKA: He just did.

EMMA: Alika, I was thinking—

ALIKA: Yeah?

EMMA: Thinking I would make an appointment with a realtor next week.

ALIKA: What for?

EMMA: To start looking.

ALIKA: What's the rush?

EMMA: We've talked about it.

ALIKA: Talking about it doesn't mean we have to do it.

EMMA: We've saved enough for the down payment.

ALIKA: This place is fine for now.

EMMA: Renting's just not the same.

ALIKA: It's fine for now.

EMMA: If we had kids, we'd need a bigger place.

ALIKA: You're not hāpai (*pregnant*), are you?

EMMA: Well no, but—

ALIKA: Thank God.

EMMA:	What do you mean thank God?
ALIKA:	I just don't want kids now.
EMMA:	But we've been married for—
ALIKA:	Look, I don't want to be saddled with a mortgage now. I don't want to come home to a house full of kids. Guys like that don't have the money or the time to enjoy life.
EMMA:	Some men *enjoy* having a family.
ALIKA:	They're always worried, worn out, or both. I have other things I want to do. I don't want that now.
EMMA:	It's what married people do—
ALIKA:	*(Escalating)* Don't push me.
EMMA:	They buy a house—
ALIKA:	We are not buying a house now!
EMMA:	They have kids.
ALIKA:	We are not having kids now!
EMMA:	When?
ALIKA:	Don't expect me to give up my life just because we're married.
EMMA:	You? What about what I'm giving up?
ALIKA:	What have you given up?
EMMA:	Listen, I've—
ALIKA:	No, you listen. I'm not ready, and I don't want to!

(ALIKA exits. Lights down.)

SCENE 8

(*CLEARWATER sits alone staring at a gun. CHORUS MAN 1 enters from behind. CLEARWATER cocks the gun.*)

CHORUS MAN 1: No, no, listen.

CLEARWATER: Why should I listen?

(*CHORUS MAN walks over to him.*)

CHORUS MAN 1: Listen to the story, my beloved son, about a Crow warrior.

CLEARWATER: I'm not a Crow.

CHORUS MAN 1: In a fight with the Sioux and Arapaho, he was hit by a large bullet, at close range, square in the chest. It tore through him, piercing his lung as it sped out through his back.

(*CLEARWATER aims the gun to his chest.*)

CLEARWATER: Death didn't frighten him. He died with honor.

CHORUS MAN 1: Ah, but he didn't die. He bled in great pain.

(*CHORUS MAN 1 takes the gun.*)

CHORUS MAN 1: But greater than the bullet pain was his remembering. The remembering of his brothers, his uncles—falling, dying before his eyes. He bled for them all.

CHORUS WOMAN 1: The men found him just outside our village.

CHORUS WOMAN 2: On his horse now shining and bathed in blood.

(*CLEARWATER becomes THE WARRIOR and CHORUS MAN 1 becomes THE WISE ONE. CHORUS MEN 2 and 3 enter to carry THE WARRIOR.*)

CHORUS WOMAN 3: With the smell of so much blood—

CHORUS WOMAN 1: We thought he must be dead.

CHORUS WOMAN 2: But the medicine man, The Wise One, ordered a brush lodge built near the river.

(*The dais becomes the brush lodge. THE WARRIOR is laid in the brush lodge.*)

CHORUS WOMAN 1: He called for silence.

CHORUS WOMAN 2: No noise.

CHORUS WOMAN 3: Quiet.

CHORUS WOMAN 1: Take care of the dogs.

CHORUS WOMAN 2: The dogs must be silent.

CHORUS WOMAN 3: And a way must be cleared.

CHORUS WOMAN 1: A way to the water.

CHORUS WOMAN 2: A way to the river that runs through our lives.

CHORUS WOMAN 3: The Wise One took his medicine bundle and entered the lodge.

(*THE CHORUS puts on wolf masks except for THE WISE ONE.*)

CHORUS MAN 2: Out of the bundle he took the skin, the skin of a wolf. The legs were stained red and the nostrils flamed red and red streaks lined the eyes and made them large and full of fire.

(*CHORUS members drum and sing.*)

CHORUS MAN 3: And we sang steadily, steadily with the voices of the drums, and he painted himself, like his medicine skin, his wolf skin. He was singing and painting his skin to his medicine song, with the drums and the people and the air afraid to breathe.

(*Pause. The drumming becomes softer and faster. THE WISE ONE puts on the wolf skin.*)

CHORUS MAN 2: And then he began to whine as the wolf mother whines for her pups. Whining he moved as the wolf moves, fretting and worrying and crying. And then as the wolf paces,

around and around the body he circled four times, whining and crying and throwing water on the fallen warrior.

(The WISE ONE circles as a wolf four times, sprinkles water with his wolf muzzle four times, and shakes a rattle four times.)

CHORUS ALL: Crying as the wolf mother cries.

(THE WARRIOR sits up as THE WISE ONE sits down like a wolf and howls four times.)

CHORUS ALL: Howling as the wolf mother howls.

(THE WARRIOR opens his eyes. THE WISE ONE stands and lifts the wolf skin over his head four times, whining and crying like a wolf mother.)

CHORUS MAN 2: Each time he lifts the skin, I am lifted.

CHORUS ALL: *(Echo)* I am lifted. I am lifted. I am lifted.

CHORUS MAN 3: Each time he lifts the skin, He is changed.

CHORUS ALL: *(Echo)* He is changed. I am changed. We are changed.

(THE WARRIOR stands on the fourth lift of the skin. CHORUS is now a pack of wolves. THE WISE ONE moves, still a wolf mother, coaxing THE WARRIOR to follow.)

CHORUS MAN 2: We are moving, moving toward the river with our brave one as once, twice, three times he falters.

(CHORUS mimics the actions of THE WISE ONE and THE WARRIOR, building.)

CHORUS WOMAN 2: Then he moves into the water, into the stream held by the singing and beating of drums. The wolf mother licking his wounds, and his blood flows black into the water and finally red, life, the red blood of life.

CHORUS WOMAN 3: And then it—

THE WISE ONE: STOP!

127

(*Quiet.*)

THE WISE ONE: (*To THE WARRIOR*) Wash yourself.

(*THE WARRIOR washes himself and follows THE WISE ONE back to the brush lodge.*)

CHORUS WOMAN 3: There they sat and smoked the pipe. In this way, the warrior lived, and wolf and man became one.

SCENE 9

(*EMMA sits alone. KAHEKA enters, and watches her.*)

EMMA: Just come in, Papa.

KAHEKA: Sorry, I can come back.

EMMA: No, come in, it's okay.

KAHEKA: I just wanted to tell you.

EMMA: Tell me what?

KAHEKA: I was thinking about what Maelyn said. I guess she's right. She's got plenty bad feelings for me.

EMMA: Me too, I guess.

KAHEKA: It's my fault. I made her like that.

EMMA: Maybe it's my fault too. I was so caught up in myself.

KAHEKA: I hope it's not too late.

EMMA: I hope so too.

KAHEKA: Emma, is something wrong?

EMMA: Alika and I, we had a fight.

KAHEKA: Oh.

EMMA: I want something he's not. He wants something I'm not.

KAHEKA: I'm sorry, Emma. I want you to be happy.

EMMA: I thought he would take her place.

KAHEKA: Whose?

EMMA: You know, when Gramma died, it was so awful.

KAHEKA: I know, baby.

EMMA: I wanted to forget so much—everything.

KAHEKA: I know.

EMMA: And now I can't remember a thing. It's like a fog and I can't see, like big pieces of my life I can't find.

KAHEKA: Someday, when the time is right.

EMMA: I pulled it all inside myself. I wanted to tie it all up in this—this, this empty dream. You tried to tell me.

KAHEKA: I told you things choose us, but—

EMMA: Will those things come back?

KAHEKA: It's really not for me to say.

(*EMMA stands silent as if far away. Enter CLEARWATER.*)

CLEARWATER: Emma, I came back because—

EMMA: Is this what you choose?

CLEARWATER: There are things we should say. We should say things and not make a big mistake.

EMMA: Sometimes I would make a mistake.

CLEARWATER: What?

EMMA: Do you know what happened when I made a mistake?

129

CLEARWATER: When?

EMMA: When I made a mistake dancing—

(CLEARWATER and KAHEKA slowly back off. KAHEKA exits, but CLEARWATER remains watching from a dim light. A CHORUS WOMAN enters as KUPUNA. She carries a plain section of wood from the trunk of a tree. It is tied with yellow kapa [bark cloth] as an image of Laka. EMMA can hear, but not see her.)

KUPUNA: Emma, Emmalehua, lei hiwahiwa (*precious child*).

EMMA: Kupuna? Kupuna wahine (*grandmother*)? I've done something wrong.

KUPUNA: *(Setting down the image, she speaks almost to herself.)* Image, we need the image of Laka, and she will come.

EMMA: Where are you?

KUPUNA: There, now take my hand.

EMMA: I don't know where you are.

KUPUNA: I can't hold on if you, if you won't take my hand.

(KUPUNA fades back and exits.)

EMMA: Where are you?! Help . . . *(Sees the image)* me.

(EMMA kneels down next to the piece of wood. Lights fade to black. Enter ALIKA, MAELYN, RICKY, GORDON, PEARL, SALLY, and JAKE. They are loud, drunk and laughing.)

MAELYN: Turn on some light, Alika.

ALIKA: I'm trying.

PEARL: Gawd it's so dark. Who did that?!!

SALLY: Jake, get off my foot.

JAKE: It's not me. It's Ricky.

RICKY: No, I'm looking for Pearl's—

PEARL:	Stop it, Ricky!
RICKY:	It's not me, it's Gordon.
GORDON:	Not! I'm using two hands to carry this case of beer.

(*The lights go bright, and they see EMMA kneeling.*)

GORDON:	Emma, what are you doing? Praying?
MAELYN:	(*Laughs*) Maybe she's cleaning the floor.
RICKY:	What's that hunk of wood?
MAELYN:	(*Looking*) Oh-oh, it's—Laka, Laka, Laka!
PEARL:	Who?
MAELYN:	A hula goddess in an old piece of wood come back to watch over her little dancer.
PEARL:	What?
MAELYN:	Just some really big secret.

(*EMMA looks at them coldly and looks away.*)

ALIKA:	Don't get sore, Emma, join the party. Have a beer.
EMMA:	I don't want a beer.
SALLY:	Could you believe those guys?
GORDON:	Yeah, Emma, you should have seen it. There was this birthday party and all these life-guards—
RICKY:	They were all dressed up like women with mu'umu'us and everything—
SALLY:	With big pillows underneath tied on their butts.
GORDON:	And giant stuffed bras—
JAKE:	Prancing all around—
SALLY:	Dancing the hula!

RICKY: Yeah, you know—*(Sings)* "Ala Moana Annie, with her enormous fanny."

PEARL: *(In response to his singing)* Oh gawd—turn on the radio!

MAELYN: Please! It's like a mausoleum in here.

(GORDON turns on the radio.)

ALIKA: Come on Emma, drink with us.

EMMA: No, I don't want to.

ALIKA: Come on.

EMMA: Leave me alone.

MAELYN: Yeah, just leave her alone, Alika. She doesn't want to have any fun.

(A hapa-haole tune comes on the radio. MAELYN does a seductive hula. She dances around ALIKA, who catches her and kisses her. MAELYN takes off her jacket and EMMA sees that she is wearing the lei hoaka. EMMA walks over, pushes ALIKA away, pulls the lei hoaka off MAELYN, and slaps her on the face.)

EMMA: How dare you!

ALIKA: Don't get jealous, Emma.

EMMA: How dare you wear this and dance that trash!

(Everyone is staring at EMMA. MAELYN runs out of the room. All party guests start to leave nervously.)

ALIKA: Hey, wait. Where are you going?

RICKY: Uh, I think we have to go.

PEARL: Look at the time!

GORDON: Yeah, we're just, we'll see you later.

ALIKA: Hey, wait a minute.

RICKY: See you folks, uh, later.

(GORDON, PEARL, JAKE, RICKY, and SALLY exit.)

ALIKA: What the hell did you do that for?

(*EMMA ignores him and takes the lei hoaka to the Laka image.*)

ALIKA: What is that doing here anyway?

EMMA: Someone brought it.

ALIKA: I know what it is, and you can get rid of it.

EMMA: I'm not going to.

ALIKA: I told you when we got married. You said—

EMMA: I've changed my mind.

ALIKA: First you get on me about a house, then you embarrass me in front of my friends, and now this hunk of wood.

EMMA: It's . . . an image.

ALIKA: Some image.

EMMA: It's better than the ones you have.

ALIKA: If you don't want to finish things here and now, then get rid of it.

EMMA: No.

ALIKA: Then I will!

(*ALIKA moves to grab the image. CLEARWATER steps out.*)

CLEARWATER: Maybe you've had too much to drink. I think you should leave that alone.

ALIKA: So what's been going on here, Emma?

CLEARWATER: Don't talk like that to her. She hasn't done anything.

ALIKA: Then get the fuck out of my house and stay away from my wife.

CLEARWATER: The way you stay away from her sister and all those other women in Waikīkī?

ALIKA: Fuck you both.

(*ALIKA moves for the image.*)

EMMA: No!

(*EMMA moves to protect the image, but ALIKA grabs her and hits her. CLEARWATER grabs ALIKA and they fight. CLEARWATER knocks ALIKA down and tears at him like an animal.*)

CLEARWATER: I said, stay away.

EMMA: Stop. Stop. Stop it now!

(*EMMA touches CLEARWATER and he backs off.*)

CLEARWATER: I'm right here. I'm right here, and I'm watch-ing you!

(*ALIKA works hard to recover himself.*)

ALIKA: Emma, Emma, you can't just do this.

EMMA: I won't erase the past and hand you the future. I won't.

ALIKA: That future, it isn't just for me.

EMMA: And what does it hold for me? For the things I love?

ALIKA: I won't be held back.

EMMA: Then I guess you'll have to make a sacrifice.

ALIKA: No, no, I know there are things I should have listened to, things I should give you.

EMMA: What is that?

ALIKA: The house, we can buy the house, and a child, your own child. I know what you need.

EMMA: Is that what *you* really want?

ALIKA: I do, Emma, I just didn't realize it before.

EMMA: (*Pause*) You'll say anything to win, won't you?

ALIKA: And you're a real loser. You just lost.

(*ALIKA exits. EMMA goes back to the image and the lei hoaka. She is quiet for a few seconds. CLEARWATER moves toward her, but she motions him off.*)

EMMA: No, no, I'm all right. (*Pause*) Mistakes, sometimes I made really bad mistakes. Do you know what would happen? When I made a mistake?

CLEARWATER: (*Softly*) I don't know.

(*KUPUNA enters.*)

KUPUNA: Emma, Emmalehua, lei hiwahiwa.

EMMA: Kupuna. Kupuna wahine.

KUPUNA: He aha ka pilikia? (*What's the trouble?*)

EMMA: Nānā ʻoe. Ua make nā mea apau. Nā maile nani, nā ʻieʻie haʻaheo, nā lauaʻe onaona, nā palapalai lahilahi. Hoʻomake au iā lākou.

   (*Look, everything's dead—the beautiful maile, the proud ʻieʻie, the fragrant lauaʻe and the delicate palapalai. I killed them.*)

KUPUNA: Mai, mai. Mai uē. Hoʻomaka hou kāua. Hoʻomaka hou ke ola. (*Come, come, don't cry. You and I will begin again. Life begins again.*) We just begin again. Take my hand now.

(*KUPUNA stretches out her hand to EMMA.*)

KUPUNA: (*Firmly*) Emma, take my hand.

(*EMMA reaches out, tentatively at first, and then takes KUPUNA'S hand in her own.*)

EMMA: I thought you'd gone away forever.

KUPUNA: Don't be silly. (*Pause*) Now where do we go, remember?

EMMA: Mauka, into the forest . . .

KUPUNA: And what do we do? No, baby, no time for tears, time is too precious, what do we do?

135

EMMA: We ask her, we ask: Ē Laka ē, ē maliu mai, Ē maliu mai 'oe, i pono au, a pono au a pono kāua. We ask you Laka, to help us, give again to us as we will give to you.

(*CHORUS enters chanting and carrying mountain greenery. They are dressed for traditional hula. EMMA and KUPUNA take some greenery, and as they chant, they build an altar.*)

CHANT: Haki pu o ka nahelehele,
Haki hana maile o ka wao,
Hooulu lei ou, o Laka, e!
O Hiiaka ke kaula nana e hooulu na ma'i,
A aeae a ulu a noho i kou kuahu,
Eia ka pule la, he pule ola,
He noi ola nou e-e!
E ola ia makou, aohe hala!

(*Pule Kuahu no Laka, traditional*)

(*This cutting of the forest,
This work of picking maile from the
wilderness,
Is to gather a lei for you, Laka.
Hi'iaka, the seer prophet, heals our ills,
Enter, possess, and live in your altar,
This is the prayer, a prayer for life.
An appeal for life.
Give us life without transgression.*)

(*CHORUS and EMMA dance. At the end of the dance EMMA comes forward.*)

EMMA: (*To CLEARWATER, warmly*) Komo mai. Come, come, you are welcome here.

CHORUS: (*They encircle CLEARWATER and EMMA*) Each time he lifts the skin, I am lifted. I am lifted. I am lifted. Each time he lifts the skin, I am changed. I am changed. We are changed.

(*CLEARWATER kisses EMMA as the lights fade to black.*)

SCENE 10

(MAELYN watches EMMA asleep on the dais. EMMA wakes up and sees MAELYN watching her.)

EMMA:	Maelyn. I'm sorry about last night. I should never have hit you. I just—
MAELYN:	Alika asked me to get his clothes.
EMMA:	*(Pause)* I had to cut it off quickly. I was never really what he thought.
MAELYN:	He wasn't exactly what you thought, believe me. Why did you ever do it in the first place?
EMMA:	Do you hate me for it?
MAELYN:	Do I hate you for it? For what? Leaving him? I would have given anything for what Gramma gave you. I would never have run away from it, especially to Alika. It scared you to carry all that, didn't it? But it wouldn't have scared me.
EMMA:	But I thought you . . . wanted him.
MAELYN:	I wanted him because he was yours. From the time we were young, I've watched and I've wanted, wanted everything you've had. I can't remember a time when I haven't felt tied to you by envy and hurt, until I was nothing, nothing but a twisted reflection of you, the one that I wasn't.
EMMA:	I'm so sorry, Mae. I know I got more than my share. *(Silence)* I'll help you get his clothes.
MAELYN:	I didn't just come because of the clothes. I came because I wanted to tell you . . . about last night. After Alika told me what happened, I was alone and still furious. I stood looking out at the moonlight through the

trees, and all of a sudden everything stopped. All the angry voices that yelled for years just stopped. It was so quiet, and I just stood there in the quiet, watching the moon sweeping over the lawn in waves, through the racing clouds, and I felt something falling off of me, like old clothes or old skin, something left me and for a moment I hardly recognized myself, standing there—as if something you finally had, or had done, released me, and I could breathe again.

(*Silence. MAELYN starts to leave. EMMA goes to her and takes her hand.*)

EMMA:	Mae.
MAELYN:	Yes.
EMMA:	When it's time, you'll come to me, and I'll teach you what she taught me. Everything. I promise.
MAELYN:	You would do that?
EMMA:	'Ae, ko'u kaikaina u'i loa (*Yes, my lovely sister*). I promise.

(*They embrace, and MAELYN exits.*)

SCENE 11

(*EMMA sits looking at the lei hoaka. CLEARWATER comes up in a spot of light.*)

EMMA:	I belong here.
CLEARWATER:	I want you. I don't want you to do this.
EMMA:	You know where you belong. It's no use arguing.

CLEARWATER: But maybe we belong together, maybe this is the way things should be—a man and a woman brought together in love by something greater than themselves. They live together and watch their children grow and their grandchildren. Maybe it's the way we should see our lives pass by.

EMMA: No, no, they raised us to take their places, and we have an obligation. We are their dreams, all of their dreams. Please don't make it harder.

(*CLEARWATER kisses EMMA.*)

EMMA: Mālama pono ku'u lei aloha. Aloha, aloha nō. (*Take care my love, goodbye, goodbye.*)

(*CLEARWATER starts to leave and turns back.*)

CLEARWATER: Remember Emma, a wolf can see far, travel all night, and never forgets his mate.

(*Exit CLEARWATER.*)

SCENE 12

(*Enter KAHEKA.*)

KAHEKA: He left?

EMMA: Yes.

KAHEKA: He's coming back?

EMMA: I told him not to.

KAHEKA: Oh.

EMMA: Did I do the right thing, Papa?

KAHEKA: You did what you thought you should.

EMMA: Sending everyone away.

139

KAHEKA: Sometimes we have to do that—let people go.

(*KAHEKA exits.*)

EMMA: Yes, I know. I remember . . .

(*EMMA moves forward as CHORUS moves around her.*)

EMMA: I remember a night when the wind came in voices through the darkness, deep and endless. They took me by the hand to the room where she lay dying, and in that room the turbulent night could not enter. It was still, so still you could hear your own heart beat. The smell of the forest and flowers drifted through the air. There were candles everywhere, and Gramma was lying there with her white hair like waves folding all around her. She looked old, yes, but through age and even dying, her warmth shone out in all its strength, binding us all together. Every once in awhile she would turn her head and talk to someone who wasn't there or to someone we couldn't see. I remember she was quiet for a long time. Then, she called me.

(*KUPUNA steps out of CHORUS.*)

KUPUNA: Emma, Emmalehua, listen, listen carefully. I'm going away now.

EMMA: You mean you're leaving me? Now?

KUPUNA: Yes.

EMMA: Everything you've taught me? After everything that's happened?

KUPUNA: There is one more thing before I leave.

(*KUPUNA places the lei hoaka over EMMA.*)

KUPUNA: This was always yours.

(*KUPUNA takes the image and gives it to one of the CHORUS.*)

KUPUNA: But this is ours. It comes from our time, and now our time is fading.

EMMA: But why? Why all of this?

KUPUNA: You make your own, for your time.

(*CHORUS repeats the chant softly as KUPUNA speaks.*)

CHORUS: 'Āmama: 'Eli'eli kapu, 'eli'eli noa. Kapu 'oukou ke akua. Noa mākou, ke kanaka.

KUPUNA: Now the kapu is done, and because it was deep, so your freedom will be something deep and new. The goddess remains kapu, but you, the woman, are free.

EMMA: Ku'u kupuna aloha (*My beloved grandmother*).

KUPUNA: 'Āmama. Ua noa (*It is finished. You are free*).

EMMA: I walked over and took her hand. She lifted my face, and her eyes, they saw so deep in me. She pulled my face close to hers, I thought to kiss me, but instead she drew in her breath and breathed out, right into my mouth.

(*CHORUS makes the soft sound of the wind. KUPUNA and CHORUS fade and exit.*)

EMMA: And it was like the mountain wind lifted me high, so high up, and placed me down again, here, and I was alone.

(*Blackout.*)

CURTAIN

OLA NĀ IWI

(The Bones Live)

FOREWORD

Ola Nā Iwi was first produced by Kumu Kahua Theatre at the Merchant Street Theatre in Honolulu on November 11, 1994. The production was directed by John H. Y. Wat, with the following cast:

Kawehi	Lyla Bonnie Berg
Erik	Jack Boyle
Mina	Karen Kaulana
Fatu	Ron Encarnacion
Gustav	Andy Mennick
Pua	Venus Kapuaala
Nanea/Liliha	Kehaunani M. Hunt
Deidre	Laura Louise Bach
Player 1	Pamela Sterling
Player 2	Craig Howes & Peter Knapman
Player 3	Jon Hamblin

Set Design: Joseph D. Dodd
Light Design: Gerald Kawaoka
Costume Design: Yvette La Fontaine

Ola Nā Iwi was commissioned by Kumu Kahua Theatre, whose activities are partially funded by the State Foundation on Culture and the Arts, State of Hawai'i.

THE CAST OF CHARACTERS

Kawehi	Part Hawaiian
Erik	Caucasian
Mina	Part Hawaiian
Fatu	Part Samoan
Gustav	German
Pua	Part Hawaiian
Nanea/Liliha	Hawaiian
Deidre	Caucasian
Player 1: Female	Mrs. Mahler, Waitress, Miss Ida, Camilla, Clown
Player 2: Male	Customs Inspector, 19th Century Southerner, 19th Century Phrenologist, Warren K. Moorehead, Clown, Dorsey
Player 3: Male	19th Century Professor 1, 19th Century Professor 2, Graverobber, Clown, Franz Boas, 19th Century Physician

THE SET

Kawehi's House is a Polynesian-looking living room with a small rattan sofa, two chairs, and a coffee table. Two exits lead to a bedroom and to the outside. In a *Playing Area Downstage* are other locations, to be suggested by minimal, moveable furniture and props, and lighting.

TIME AND PLACE

The play is set in Berlin and Honolulu. The time is the present, except for brief historical interludes.

Act I

SCENE 1

(*Honolulu. A CUSTOMS INSPECTOR stands behind a table. Enter KAWEHI. She places two bags on the table and hands him her papers.*)

INSPECTOR: Where are you traveling from, ma'am?

KAWEHI: Berlin.

INSPECTOR: (*Looking in passport*) Berlin?

KAWEHI: London. Sorry, I spent the night in London. I must be really tired.

INSPECTOR: How long were you in Germany?

KAWEHI: Two weeks.

INSPECTOR: Vacation?

KAWEHI: Half a vacation. I was with the 'Aulama Theatre at the Berliner Theatre Festival.

INSPECTOR: Did I read about that somewhere?

KAWEHI: Yeah, we did *Hamlet.*

INSPECTOR: No food items, plants, nothing to declare?

KAWEHI: Nope, just clothes and some props.

INSPECTOR:	Are you an actress?
KAWEHI:	I was just a stagehand, and a kind of consultant.
INSPECTOR:	Consultant? Could you open your bags please?
KAWEHI:	Sure. *(Unzips bags)* A cultural consultant.
INSPECTOR:	Where do you work?
KAWEHI:	Oh, I'm a teacher.
INSPECTOR:	Teacher?
KAWEHI:	I'm on sabbatical.
INSPECTOR:	*(Pulls out a Hawaiian pūloʻuloʻu stick)* This doesn't look German.
KAWEHI:	The play was set in pre-contact Hawaiʻi. I helped research and supervise the reproduction of artifacts. Looks real, doesn't it?

(THE INSPECTOR brings out a skull.)

INSPECTOR:	Alas, poor Yorick?
KAWEHI:	That's poor Keaka. You like Shakespeare?
INSPECTOR:	I played Laertes in high school.
KAWEHI:	Did you go to high school here in Honolulu? Maybe I saw you.
INSPECTOR:	No. Annandale, Virginia. This looks so real.
KAWEHI:	We had a whole set of bones made just for the show. I had to pack it in my clothes to protect it. Careful! They cost a small fortune.
INSPECTOR:	*(Carefully wrapping it up)* You sure you don't act?
KAWEHI:	*(Smiling)* Well, every once and a while.
INSPECTOR:	I was thinking about getting back into it.

KAWEHI:	*(Taking the skull from his hands)* Oh, you should. You really should. It's a great release. I bet this job can be stressful.
INSPECTOR:	Don't I know it. You can't believe what people try to smuggle in their bags. Just the other day there was guy with a tarantula.
KAWEHI:	A tarantula?
INSPECTOR:	Yeah, just running around in his suitcase, not even in a jar or anything.
KAWEHI:	Are mine okay?
INSPECTOR:	Huh?
KAWEHI:	My bags, I mean.
INSPECTOR:	*(Gives back her passport)* Oh, sure. Just follow the green line out. Maybe I'll see you on the stage.
KAWEHI:	I hope I see *you* there.
INSPECTOR:	Have a nice day.

SCENE 2

(Berlin. An Office. ERIK JAMISON, an American, and MRS. MAHLER, a German.)

ERIK:	No, I don't know anyone like that, Mrs. Mahler.
MRS. MAHLER:	You are sure?
ERIK:	I haven't even run into anyone here in Berlin from the south.
MRS. MAHLER:	That is what she told Dr. Heinrich at the museum. An anthropologist from the south. He said she had, how do you say it, a charming southern drool.

149

ERIK:	That's drawl, southern drawl.
MRS. MAHLER:	Drawl. But maybe it's an imitation.
ERIK:	I don't understand what the police think this has to do with our production.
MRS. MAHLER:	It is because of the nature of the missing items.
ERIK:	What's that?
MRS. MAHLER:	Valuable archaeological specimens.
ERIK:	What was it? Jewelry, sculpture?
MRS. MAHLER:	Human remains.
ERIK:	Bones?
MRS. MAHLER:	Hawaiian.
ERIK:	Oh.
MRS. MAHLER:	So, you see, you were a large group from Hawai'i.
ERIK:	Naturally. When did this happen?
MRS. MAHLER:	Two nights ago. Tuesday.
ERIK:	The cast left Berlin on Sunday. I've just been resting.
MRS. MAHLER:	Here is the artist's drawing. You are sure you've not met such a woman?
ERIK:	Positive.
MRS. MAHLER:	The museum is most anxious. It doesn't want, well, ideas to spread.
ERIK:	Ideas?
MRS. MAHLER:	The museum holds things from many countries and cultures. What would we do if everyone wanted everything back?
ERIK:	I see. Whose were they?

MRS. MAHLER:	Pardon?
ERIK:	The bones?
MRS. MAHLER:	Some native specimen. Well over 100 years old.
ERIK:	Kept for?
MRS. MAHLER:	Research and exhibit, Mr. Jamison. That is what we do, research and exhibit.
ERIK:	Look, we just came to do a play at the festival. I don't know anything about this person or the incident.
MRS. MAHLER	Not an incident, a *theft*, Mr. Jamison.
ERIK:	I know nothing about it.
MRS. MAHLER:	You will be in Germany long?
ERIK:	I leave tomorrow.
MRS. MAHLER:	You will leave information, in case we need to contact you?
ERIK:	Certainly, but I don't imagine I could be of any help. *(Short pause)* If that's all, I'd like to be going, Mrs. Mahler. I have some business at the theatre, and I need to pack, say goodbye to friends, you know.
MRS. MAHLER:	Of course. I understand, Mr. Jamison. Thank you for your time.
ERIK:	*(Exiting)* Good day.
MRS. MAHLER:	Good day. *(After a pause)* You can come now, Gustav.

(Enter GUSTAV.)

MRS. MAHLER:	What do you think?
GUSTAV:	Could be he's telling the truth. Could be he's lying. Who knows, he's in the theatre.
MRS. MAHLER:	I used to do some theatrical work.

GUSTAV:	You gave it up?
MRS. MAHLER:	When I married. My husband is very conservative. He enjoys watching, but feels that participating invites promiscuity.
GUSTAV:	I see.
MRS. MAHLER:	He's a liar, of course.
GUSTAV:	Your husband?
MRS. MAHLER:	No, no, this Jamison fellow! Someone at the theatre has seen him with the woman.
GUSTAV:	Why did you—
MRS. MAHLER:	We need to find *her*. *She* has the artifacts. I'm afraid this means you will have to follow him.
GUSTAV:	You mean, in the middle of winter you want me to leave Berlin and—
MRS. MAHLER:	Yes! Go to Hawai'i!
GUSTAV:	*Ach du mein Gott!*
MRS. MAHLER:	And no publicity. If this were made public, it would only create sympathy for the other side.
GUSTAV:	How will I manage if I can't use the police? I know no one there.
MRS. MAHLER:	We have help for you. Scotland Yard owes us for—well they owe us. They've asked an inspector on leave to help us, someone with native blood, who understands the islands.
GUSTAV:	*(Jokes)* Who is it? Charlie Chan?
MRS. MAHLER:	He'll contact you in Honolulu. His name is Mr., Mr., *(She puzzles over it, has trouble pronouncing it)* Fat-you!

SCENE 3

(Playing Area. A NINETEENTH CENTURY PROFESSOR.)

PROFESSOR: Doubts, there are those who raise doubts to the fact that the human species is descended from a single pair. In most instances, these objectors point to the weak intellects and savage customs of barbarous peoples. But with the dawning of the new nineteenth century comes the enlightened explanation to these doubts. Through modern scientific thought, we now recognize the astounding effects of the *environment* on the development of the human species. Environments determine not only our physical appearance, but our character, customs, and intellect as well. Our own advanced civilization abounds with innumerable stimuli of a civilized, scientific, educational and religious nature. The weak intellect of the savage is due to the want of these stimuli. Our studies positively conclude that through the manipulation of environmental influences it is possible to mold the savage into an acceptable civilized form. And these practices are underway right now with the missions to the heathens. Yes! With teachings of our enlightened civilization, we *can* actually change them culturally and physically! Isn't it wonderful?

(Playing Area. A NINETEENTH CENTURY SOUTHERNER.)

SOUTHERNER: All very well in theory sir, you and your Philosophical Society are all very well in theory but let us look toward the facts. Could anyone possibly think that the whole human race is descended from a single pair? Do we, gentlemen, at all resemble the dark and savage races which inhabit the remote areas of the globe? Now, it might be nice to think that we could raise up the barbarians of the world to a state of Christian civilization, but the fact is they were born into a low mental state, and they will die that way. Whether we expose them to all the benefits of civilization or not, we cannot change their essential nature. Take as an example, if you will, the child-like African, who has shown only slight progress under slavery and after over one hundred years. The American Indian does not flower under civilization. On the contrary, he withers up and dies. The truth is that non-white races are inferior in every way, and will never advance. They must either be kept in slavery, or allowed to become extinct, in order to make way for progress.

SCENE 4

(*Kawehi's House. KAWEHI and ERIK.*)

KAWEHI: (*With a fake southern accent*) And so I said, "I so admire your progressive paper, Dr. Heinrich, 'Measurement Variations in the Rocker Jaw of Pre-Contact Hawaiians between 1720 and 1721,' and I've heard you have the most fascinating bone collection here!"

ERIK: Why did you do it, Kawehi?

KAWEHI: I don't know, Erik. One thing just led to another. Maybe I was tired, tired of all the *talk* about things being returned to us. Who knows? I just did it, and now it's done.

ERIK: You know, I think maybe somebody's watching us!

KAWEHI:	What?
ERIK:	I heard noises outside the window awhile ago.
KAWEHI:	Did you *see* anybody?
ERIK:	I thought I saw some shadows.
KAWEHI:	Maybe you should go upstairs to your place and try to get some sleep. I think you've got jet lag.
ERIK:	Will you come with me?
KAWEHI:	No.
ERIK:	Why not?
KAWEHI:	Because I have to figure out what to do with the, you know, my little parcel.
ERIK:	Where are they?
KAWEHI:	Under the bed.
ERIK:	Ugh.
KAWEHI:	What do you mean, ugh?
ERIK:	Well, I guess it's perfectly normal for you to have a strange skeleton under your bed. I should just shut up.
KAWEHI:	Don't get weird just because I'm not going to sleep with you tonight.
ERIK:	Hey, you were the one who told me those creepy stories about spirits hanging around their bones.
KAWEHI:	Come on, Erik, I need to take it somewhere, give it a decent burial. That person was Hawaiian. Some asshole graverobber stole those bones. They couldn't even leave us alone after we were dead. Those kūpuna *(elders)* should all come home, every single one of them.

ERIK: I know how *you* feel about it, love, but international robbery and skeletons under the bed make *me* a little nervous.

KAWEHI: Are the prop bones safe?

ERIK: They were shipped with the set. I have them at the theatre.

(*A loud sound from outside. KAWEHI and ERIK both jump.*)

ERIK: Oh shit. I told you someone's out there.

KAWEHI: Go look!

ERIK: Me? You go look. They might not want to hurt a woman.

(*KAWEHI makes a face and tiptoes over to the window and looks out.*)

KAWEHI: There's nothing but the neighbor's cat.

ERIK: Maybe you could give them to that group that takes care of reburial.

KAWEHI: Maybe.

ERIK: When?

KAWEHI: When I want to.

ERIK: Kawehi—

KAWEHI: I said I would.

ERIK: But when?

KAWEHI: I just want to keep them for awhile.

ERIK: Why?

KAWEHI: I don't know. I took a big risk for them.

ERIK: Taking, you're *taking* a big risk. I told you those museum people want them back pretty bad. They've got people looking for you.

KAWEHI: So? You told them you didn't know me.

ERIK: Maybe they believed me, maybe they didn't. You know I'm taking a big risk too. It's called withholding evidence.

KAWEHI: I saw that box, and I *had* to do it.

ERIK: You know, I think you just need to take a break, Kawehi. You've plowed through the last ten years like a steamroller. Your mother just died. Look, you don't *have* to work for awhile. Couldn't you just take some time off?

KAWEHI: I don't really have a job to go back to anyway.

ERIK: What?

KAWEHI: While I was away, Pua's made a few changes. She's terminated four out of the five positions in our department, redefined them, and we all have to reapply. It's called restructuring.

ERIK: You've been there twice as long. You were offered her job.

KAWEHI: I hate administrative work. I want to work on exhibits.

ERIK: She's too much.

KAWEHI: You're telling me. I have to talk to her this week, and it might not be pretty.

ERIK: *(Getting up to leave)* Yeah, so won't you come up and spend the night with me?

KAWEHI: When I want to sleep with you every night, I'll marry you. Okay?

ERIK: Promise?

KAWEHI: Maybe.

ERIK: Try to relax and have a peaceful night.

(ERIK kisses KAWEHI and exits. KAWEHI starts to straighten up and hears a noise like a voice. She stops, listens, and continues. She hears the noise again. There is a soft tapping and a female voice.)

VOICE: Please, let me in.

KAWEHI: Who's there?

VOICE: Please let me in. I'm so cold.

(KAWEHI moves to the door.)

KAWEHI: Who is it?

VOICE: So cold out here. Please help me.

(Silence. KAWEHI hesitates, pulls open the door.)

KAWEHI: Oh, my god!

(KAWEHI exits.)

KAWEHI: (Off stage) You're like ice.

(KAWEHI enters with NANEA. NANEA is shivering and cold, with torn clothes. KAWEHI steers her over to the sofa.)

KAWEHI: Are you crazy? You can't wander around like this.

NANEA: Please, I'm so cold.

KAWEHI: What happened?

NANEA: Everything. They took everything and left me.

KAWEHI: Who?

NANEA: Somehow I got back. I just came back. I don't know, don't know anyone.

(KAWEHI gets a blanket and puts it over her.)

KAWEHI: Are you hurt? Did they hurt you? Maybe I should call an ambulance.

NANEA: What?

KAWEHI: A doctor.

NANEA: No, please, no doctor.

KAWEHI: But I think you're ill.

NANEA:	Doctor, ambulance, maybe police. No, I don't think you'd like police either.
KAWEHI:	Why do you say that?
NANEA:	Why do you think?
KAWEHI:	What are you doing here?
NANEA:	You have something, don't you?
KAWEHI:	What do you mean?
NANEA:	It's under your bed.
KAWEHI:	Who are you?
NANEA:	Call me Nanea.

SCENE 5

(*A Waikīkī hotel bar. FATU and GUSTAV.*)

FATU:	My name's pronounced "Fah-Too" not "Fat-You."
GUSTAV:	Sorry, Fatu, these Hawaiian words are difficult for me.
FATU:	Samoan, my father was half-Samoan.
GUSTAV:	I was under the impression you were born *here.*
FATU:	No. Apia, Samoa. I work now in London.
GUSTAV:	You're a long way from home.
FATU:	My mother's from London. She was an anthropologist for the British Museum.
GUSTAV:	Ah, then you understand the value of the missing artifacts.

FATU:	I know why you want them back, yes. Germany holds quite a collection of Polynesian remains and artifacts.

(Enter a WAITRESS in a raffia hula skirt and sequined bra-top.)

WAITRESS:	Good evening, welcome to our Aloha Nui Lounge. Can I take your order?
GUSTAV:	I think I will try this "Planter's Punch."
FATU:	Glenlivet, neat, please.
GUSTAV:	*(To waitress)* Is this a native costume you are wearing?
FATU:	It's a costume, my friend, not native to anything.
WAITRESS:	Don't you like it?
FATU:	*(Embarrassed)* Well, to tell you the truth, no, I don't.
WAITRESS:	Why don't you complain to the management about it? I don't like it either.
GUSTAV:	Why wear it?
WAITRESS:	Well sir, all I have right now is a high school diploma. If you could find me a politically correct job that pays this much I'd be happy to take *that*, but in the meantime this "costume" supports two kids.

(Exit WAITRESS. Enter MINA. She is dressed tastefully.)

FATU:	Ah, Mina, welcome.
MINA:	*(Kisses him on the cheek)* Tālofa lava *(greetings)*, Fatu.
FATU:	Mina, this is Gustav, whom we'll be assisting. Gustav, this is the private investigator I've engaged to work on your behalf, Mina Beckley. I've worked with Mina many times before. As I told you, she is extremely good.

MINA:	Besides, I'm his second, or is it third cousin?
GUSTAV:	Inspector Fatu has told you how we will rely on your utmost discretion.
MINA:	I couldn't afford to be in this business if I wasn't discrete. I've located Jamison.
GUSTAV:	So soon?
MINA:	If you're interested in theatre, you know him. He's one of the only innovative directors on the island.
FATU:	*(Slightly flirtatious)* Are you interested?
MINA:	Umm-Hmm.
FATU:	My grandfather wrote several plays.
MINA:	The famous Inspector Fatu wrote plays?
FATU:	As opposed to his undistinguished grandson?
MINA:	Sorry, Fatu.
FATU:	They were never produced. He hid them away, but I've read them. I think they're quite good.
MINA:	Could I read them sometime? I know a small theatre, always looking for new scripts.
GUSTAV:	*(Trying to interrupt)* Could we please? Oh—

(*WAITRESS enters with two drinks.*)

WAITRESS:	There you are.
GUSTAV:	Ah ha! Very fancy.
FATU:	*(To WAITRESS)* I hope I haven't offended you. I was very insensitive.
WAITRESS:	It's okay. Forget it. Ma'am, can I get you something?
MINA:	I'd like an Old-Fashioned please.

(*Exit WAITRESS.*)

GUSTAV:	So you've located Jamison?
MINA:	Yes, and there's a woman living in the flat just underneath his—
FATU:	Girlfriend?
MINA:	I think so.
GUSTAV:	Is it her?
MINA:	Could be.
GUSTAV:	Good, let's talk to her.
FATU:	Now, slow down. You know, Gustav, Hawaiians often work together very closely. If she suspects—
MINA:	It might not even be her. All we have is the artist's drawing.
FATU:	If she suspects—
MINA:	And even if it *is* her, the bones might not be there.
FATU:	If she suspects, she could dispose of them like that, and you'd never see them.

(*WAITRESS returns with MINA'S drink and exits.*)

MINA:	I think we should get in there some other way, make friends and—
FATU:	Yes, Mina is right. I agree, gather more information.
GUSTAV:	(*Trying an American accent*) Size them up, buster!
MINA:	Let Fatu and I check things out. You could have a little vacation in the meantime. There's a party at the theatre next week which I'm sure they'll be at. We'll all go to that.
GUSTAV:	I think it's better they don't see me.
MINA:	They won't see any of us. It's a costume party.

FATU: Mina, you're wonderful.

GUSTAV: Perhaps I will go on a historical walking tour. There are several of them I would like to see.

MINA: Those "Take You Back in Time" walks?

GUSTAV: Yes, and I would like to go swimming in the Pacific Ocean while I am here. I might never get another opportunity.

MINA: The beach is quite nice right in front of the hotel here.

FATU: We can finish talking at dinner. You have a swim, and we'll meet you in the lobby at seven.

GUSTAV: Yes, yes, you've read my mind exactly. Thank you, yes I will go now, and we will talk more at dinner. Charmed to meet you, Miss Mina.

(*Exit GUSTAV.*)

FATU: I told you he wouldn't be much trouble.

MINA: So far.

FATU: Have you made contact with the woman?

MINA: Not yet. There's a complication.

FATU: Someone else has shown up?

MINA: I think so. Your mother said something like this might happen.

FATU: That was awfully fast.

MINA: This is way more complicated than those other artifacts. We'll have to keep Gustav away until we're sure. He could mess things up.

FATU: Do you want me to call mother in now?

MINA: Not now, but I want to know who that is and what's going on.

 163

FATU: I'll ask her. *(Pause, amused)* Are we really going to a costume party?

MINA: It's characters from Shakespeare, in honor of the Berlin performance.

FATU: Great, Gustav can go in drag as Ophelia.

MINA: Don't be mean. I'll have a costume for you too.

(*WAITRESS comes in.*)

WAITRESS: Would anyone care for another drink?

FATU: *(Looks at WAITRESS)* I have to wear a costume too?

WAITRESS: You can borrow mine.

SCENE 6

(*Kawehi's House. KAWEHI and ERIK.*)

ERIK: Wait a minute. First she tells you she's been away for a long time, and now you're saying she's landed a job in two days?

KAWEHI: Yep. She has a costume and everything. Some kind of historic tour downtown.

ERIK: How does she explain showing up naked and knowing about the bones?

KAWEHI: I don't want to pressure her. She seems a little mixed up.

ERIK: Great, now there's a crazed woman *and* a skeleton.

KAWEHI: *(Defensive)* You haven't even met her. She's not crazy. She's had some kind of trauma. She's . . . just vulnerable, that's all.

ERIK: (*Accusing*) You *like* her.

KAWEHI: I want to be compassionate.

ERIK: That doesn't mean foolish.

KAWEHI: Besides, we have to be nice to her. She *knows*.

ERIK: Better find out what her game is—fast.

(*Enter NANEA with a shopping bag.*)

NANEA: Aloha awakea (*good afternoon*), Kawehi.

KAWEHI: Aloha nō (*greetings*). Where have you been?

NANEA: Out. I used your clothes again. I hope you don't mind. I'll have my own soon.

KAWEHI: Nanea, this is my friend, Erik.

NANEA: How nice to meet a friend of Kawehi's. Look, I have all this food, beer, and I got this packet of 'awa (*kava*), all ground up. Isn't it clever? Let's eat.

(*NANEA takes out all kinds of Hawaiian food and beer.*)

NANEA: Here, have a beer. (*Pause*) What a kind face you have, Erik.

ERIK: (*Embarrassed*) Well, thank you. Thank you.

KAWEHI: Erik is the artistic director for the 'Aulama Theatre.

NANEA: I love plays. Once when I was a girl, this wild Englishman built this theatre set in—where I was living—and he made this forest and a castle out of kapa (*bark cloth*) that was cut and dyed. He even made a bamboo cannon, and in one scene that was supposed to be a battle, he fired the little cannon but it missed its mark, and set the kapa castle and forest on fire. We laughed so much.

ERIK: That sounds dangerous.

KAWEHI: Where was this?

NANEA: Oh, it was so long ago. . . . Eat, eat. . . .

KAWEHI: Nanea, how did you pay for this?

NANEA: The man just gave it to me.

ERIK: You're kidding.

NANEA: No, he and I spent a long time speaking in Hawaiian. He loved the way I talk, and I loved talking to him. You know, it's been a long time. . . .

(*NANEA stops and stares as if far away.*)

KAWEHI: Since?

NANEA: What?

KAWEHI: It's been a long time since—

NANEA: (*Sadly*) Since, well, since I've had anyone to speak with.

(*Pause. ERIK and KAWEHI look at her and each other.*)

KAWEHI: (*Moving to comfort her*) Hey, it's all right. We all feel a terrible loss. It's one of the things that binds us together.

NANEA: Loss, that must be it. All that loss, and then to be home.

KAWEHI: I don't know what you've been through, but if you're in any trouble, I'll help you.

NANEA: Kind, you're so kind.

KAWEHI: Erik will too. (*Pause*) Won't you, Erik?

ERIK: Sure, sure I will.

SCENE 7

(Playing Area. Enter a NINETEENTH CENTURY PROFESSOR.)

PROFESSOR: Now, with the modern scientific research of the 1850s into the questions of racial origins and differences, modern investigators conclude that the comparison of *crania* is a principal requisite to such inquiries. Mr. Camper, the renowned anatomist, asserts that some races are closer to primates. His theory rests on the facial angle that measures the degree to which the lower jaw protrudes from the face. This protrusion is more pronounced in apes and non-white races alike, and stands as scientific evidence that such races are, indeed, closer to primates and hence, more primitive. Furthermore, there are certain important points, gentlemen, that we must remember in our investigations. One, that each race possesses a uniquely shaped skull; two, that skulls do not reflect environmental influences, and therefore provide a more accurate index of racial capabilities; three, that cranial measurements indicate brain size and therefore intelligence; four, that we will have to acquire for our study numerous skulls for the advancement of this new and most important science, craniology.

SCENE 8

(An Office. KAWEHI put files in a box. Enter PUA.)

PUA: Packing?

KAWEHI: That's right, Pua.

PUA: I got your application.

KAWEHI: Good.

PUA: To tell you the truth, I didn't like your exhibit on the Wailele site. In fact, I'm taking it down from the gallery.

KAWEHI: I did an exhibit based on archaeological evidence and oral history.

PUA: Flimsy archaeological evidence.

KAWEHI: Oral history is valid evidence.

PUA: You have absolutely no proof there was a heiau *(temple)* there.

KAWEHI: That history was meticulously handed down for hundreds of years. More than one chant names that place as the site of a luakini heiau.

PUA: And you drew too much attention to human sacrifice.

KAWEHI: I *explained* it. Pretending we were pristine and perfect makes us look foolish.

PUA: Our culture was great. I guess you don't think that, Kawehi.

KAWEHI: You know I do. I just don't have to pretend it was perfect to love it.

PUA: Well, you can apply for the position if you want, but I should warn you, you'll have some competition. And I'm carefully considering everyone's attitude.

KAWEHI: The Wailele site is on the verge of resort development.

PUA: Attitude, I don't want anyone with a racist attitude.

KAWEHI: What are you talking about?

PUA: As a native Hawaiian in this position, I have to make sure that Hawaiian history is portrayed correctly and accurately by people who care.

KAWEHI: By you and a House of Un-Hawaiian Activities.

PUA: It's not un-Hawaiian to protect the culture from misinformation.

(*Pause. KAWEHI stares at PUA.*)

KAWEHI: It's true, isn't it? (*Pause*) You're in bed with the developers.

PUA: My only concern is for the Hawaiian people.

KAWEHI: Don't do it, Pua.

PUA: Development brings money and jobs to a community.

KAWEHI: (*Sarcastic*) Right, Pua, and Waikīkī's made Hawaiians into millionaires. (*Pause*) You're afraid my research will get in the way.

PUA: You are a nobody. I've been a leader in the Hawaiian movement from the very beginning!

KAWEHI: And you're making sure it pays off.

PUA: (*Threatening*) Don't talk to me like that.

KAWEHI: I don't want to talk to you at all.

PUA: Good, because you're never going to work here again.

KAWEHI: I could go to the Board of Directors about this.

PUA: I've already had a talk with them.

KAWEHI: About donations from the developer?

PUA: They're smart.

KAWEHI:	I could go to the press.
PUA:	I could too.
KAWEHI:	You don't speak for everybody.
PUA:	But when I talk, more people listen.
KAWEHI:	That's because you talk out of both sides of your mouth.

(*Blackout.*)

SCENE 9

(*A NINETEENTH CENTURY PHRENOLOGIST and his assistant MISS IDA enter the Playing Area.*)

PHRENOLOGIST: Welcome, welcome, welcome to all you good gentlemen of Pinhead. I am the good Reverend, Dr. Pinchbottom, and here's my lovely assistant, Miss Ida. I come before you today, gentlemen, to testify to you, that just as the feathers identify the bird, just as the flowers foretell the fruit, just as the map reveals the lay of the land, I tell you today, good gentlemen of the town of Pinhead, that phrenology, that's p-h-r / e-n-o / l-o-g-y, phrenology, has been given to mankind to unfold the mysteries of life. I swear to you truly, on my soul, on my honor, on my deep love of God, this marvelous new science holds the key to a better life—free of sickness, free of crime, free of pain, personal calamity, bad choices, bad marriages, bad business, bad crops, and bad breath. Miss Ida, please. (*MISS IDA rolls down a phrenology chart*) Now as we see here, the brain is simply a big muscle, and like a muscle, those parts which we exercise become larger, as a muscle would become larger through frequent exercising. And as you can all see by this scientific chart, different muscles of the brain control different traits. Note here the areas of intelligence, health, conviviality, and criminality. Now sir, step up here for a moment, and let Miss Ida roll up your sleeve. That's it, now would you be so kind as to flex that arm for Miss Ida. Now Miss Ida, I want you to feel those muscles on the gentleman's arm. Can you feel them? Now, just as Miss Ida can feel those rippling muscles, so can I, by examining the lumps, the bumps, and the organic contours of your head, so can I reveal to you your true nature, according to the muscles of your brain which you have, and have not, given to exercise. I can read your tendencies, your flagrancies, your miseries, and your jealousies. I can tell your good habits, bad habits, and habits you wish you had, your strong parts, weak parts, and your parts unknown. I can even help you to find true love, or just a little you-know-what, through my modern scientific training in the marvelous, miracle science of phrenology. Remember now, the finger of divine providence may point the way to your golden opportunities, but it is up to you to follow. Now who'll be the first to line right up for only one dollar and receive the light of new knowledge? I should add, that this dollar includes, unique to the Pinchbottom method of phrenology only, the Universal Current Enhancing Phrenology Massage, by the lovely Miss Ida—guaranteed to bring out the best in your potential. Now don't push, gentlemen, and start lining up right here. I said, don't push!

(*Blackout, then lights up to half.*)

PHRENOLOGIST: (*quieter*) Oh yes, I almost forgot. In order to advance this wonderful study of phrenology, there are many, many, scholars in need of skulls for their scientific investigations, especially skulls from the various heathen tribes. All those interested in the financial rewards of promoting this worthy science by providing specimens please see me—tonight.

SCENE 10

(*MINA'S House. MINA and FATU sprinkle themselves with a ti leaf and salt water.*)

MINA: Quit whining, Fatu.

FATU: It drives me crazy when my mother wants me to do this weird stuff.

MINA: Don't be a wimp, a little salt water won't hurt you.

FATU: If we were in my father's village, Mina, you'd be more respectful.

MINA: Cooperate, or I'll tell your mother.

FATU: She's so—superstitious.

MINA: What!?

FATU: Tulou lava (*excuse me*). *Traditional.* And that fax she sent—bones, chiefess, high rank—such inefficient communication.

MINA: You're quite the fussy pālagi (*Caucasian*) these days.

FATU: O a'u Samoa (*I'm Samoan*).

MINA: Then just do what she says—anytime we go near the house or near anyone that comes in and out of it. And she said to keep a ti leaf on us too.

FATU: Okaoka *(oh my)*, these primitive rituals!

MINA: Still remember how to tail someone?

FATU: Can I tail you?

MINA: I *am* going to tell your mother.

FATU: I can't help it. You island women just make my hot Polynesian blood boil.

MINA: Shut up, Fatu.

SCENE 11

(Playing Area. NANEA in a nineteenth century dress. GUSTAV stands as if part of an audience. MINA and FATU watch from a distance.)

NANEA: Here we are at Kawaiaha'o church, symbol of the new religion of Christianity in nineteenth century Hawai'i. Many of the chiefs joined the church and attended services here. But some of the chiefs felt oppressed by the new laws, Christianity, and the casting off of all that was sacred. When the chief Boki decided to show his allegiance to Kauikeaouli, Kamehameha the Third, in the old way, he gave him all his Hilo lands to divide up as he saw fit. It angered Ka'ahumanu and the other Christian chiefs, for she took it as a sign that Boki rebelled against *her* authority. When she announced that the government would assume the sandalwood debts of all chiefs, she excluded Boki and insulted him by making

173

him the only chief responsible for his own debt. Then, Ka'ahumanu did a thing which Boki could never forgive or forget. A thing which, whenever he thought of it, plagued his heart and tore at him from the inside. In January of the year 1829, to prove her loyalty to the Christian faith, and to assert her authority, Ka'ahumanu went, accompanied by some of the missionaries, to Hale o Keawe, where the sacred bones of our chiefs lay. Some of the bones she gathered up and moved to the caves in the cliffs above Ka'awaloa. The rest she burned. Many people heaped her name with abuse for this supreme insult to the bones of departed chiefs. "The bones of our chiefs should be well cared for," shouted Boki, "Instead, she breaks down Hale o Keawe, shows the hidden bones of the chiefs in public, and burns the others." "Perhaps," he cried, "if she knew where Kamehameha's bones lay, she would show them in public too."

(*Lights to half on MINA and FATU.*)

FATU: I've seen that face before.

MINA: She's absolutely magnetic.

FATU: I'm telling you, I know I've seen her face before.

(*Lights fade on MINA and FATU.*)

NANEA: And Boki heard there was sandalwood in the New Hebrides. He dreamt of cutting enough sandalwood to clear his debt. The trees came crashing down in his dreams, log after log, enough to erase the entire debt of the nation. In his dreams, he returned wrapped in the sweet scent of sandalwood and foreign money —a hero, a chief greater than Ka'ahumanu.

He placed his land and authority in the hands of his wife, Liliha, and to the laments and pleas of those who loved him, he sailed away with his dream. *(Pause)* Liliha never saw him again. His bones would be lost, never to return to rest in his homeland.

(*GUSTAV claps and approaches NANEA.*)

GUSTAV: Excuse me, I wish to ask why was it so upsetting to burn these bones?

NANEA: We believe that the spirit, the essence, the mana *(spiritual power)* resides in the bones. If not properly hidden or cared for in the old way, the spirit of the departed one is forced to wander, unhappy and restless, never finding its way to the ao 'aumākua, the realm of the ancestors, never finding home. No peace.

GUSTAV: I see. I have learned so much about your history tonight, and I wish to tell you, you were, how do you say in English, enchanting?

NANEA: Yes, enchanting.

GUSTAV: *Sprechen Sie deutsch?*

NANEA: *Ja, ein bisschen.*

GUSTAV: It's lucky for me they picked you for this job.

NANEA: I'm glad you think so.

GUSTAV: History is a fascinating study, and all the things connected with it. So important.

NANEA: German history is very interesting too.

GUSTAV: *Vielleicht könnten wir zusammen kaffee trinken gehen und etwas plaudern?*

NANEA: *Ja, jetzt.*

(*Exit NANEA and GUSTAV.*)

MINA: Did you hear that?

175

FATU: What's going on here?

MINA: So you thought Gustav was harmless and easy to handle?

FATU: I don't know. Maybe she just speaks German.

MINA: "Lucky for me they picked you for this job"?

SCENE 12

(*Kawehi's House. ERIK and KAWEHI.*)

ERIK: And there she was, drinking coffee with this German guy and chatting away.

KAWEHI: So?

ERIK: In German.

KAWEHI: So she speaks German.

ERIK: You have this blind trust. How do you know what she's getting us into?

KAWEHI: I don't want to hear this.

ERIK: Wake up, Kawehi. You take those, those, you know—

KAWEHI: They're called bones.

ERIK: You take those bones from Berlin. You know they're looking for you. She appears a few days later, knows about them, and just happens to speak German.

KAWEHI: I just don't think she's like that.

ERIK: Look, if you don't care about being caught and arrested for your noble cause, fine. But I don't want to be entrapped.

KAWEHI: What do you want me to do?

ERIK: *(Escalating)* I want you to see what's going on. I want you to be a little more suspicious. I want you to be a little more cautious. I want you to develop some kind of awareness of the position she's putting us in.

KAWEHI: *(Yelling)* If she's what you say, why hasn't she just had me arrested?

ERIK: I don't know! You're risking everything for some bones. That person is dead and gone. I'm trying to be patient. I'm trying to understand, but I just don't.

KAWEHI: Maybe you can't because—

ERIK: Because? Because? Go ahead and say it. Because I'm not Hawaiian?

(*Exit ERIK. Lights out.*)

SCENE 13

(*Playing Area. A GRAVEROBBER steps into light.*)

GRAVEROBBER: You ask about my manner of collecting? Their burial places are in plain sight of many Indian houses not far from the fort, and very near frequented roads. I wait until the dead of night, when not even the dogs are stirring. After securing a skull, I then have to pass the Indian sentry at the stockade gate, so I never enter with more than one at a time underneath my coat. The male skull of the old Indian I send you died at the fort on January 7th, 1869. I secured his head the night of the day he was buried. He was laid to rest in his blankets and furs in the usual place, about a half a mile from the fort. Now there is a growing suspicion among them about me, and I knew that it was their intention to watch over the body. Believing probably that I would never steal his head before he was cold in his grave, they did not keep watch the first night, and thus myself and my two hospital attendants easily secured this fine specimen for you. Perhaps you might decide sometime to honor me as a collector and display it.

SCENE 14

(*Kawehi's House. Soft lights. A roll of sennit cord is on the table. NANEA is mixing awa in a bowl.*)

KAWEHI: What's the sennit for?

NANEA: We need to weave a kā'ai, a casket for the bones.

KAWEHI: No one knows how to make those.

NANEA: I do.

KAWEHI: How?

NANEA: Watching the kūpuna.

KAWEHI: What kūpuna?

NANEA: My kūpuna. It's a family secret.

KAWEHI: Is it going to take a long time to make?

NANEA: Would that bother you?

KAWEHI: (*Uncertain, uncomfortable*) I'm just asking how—

NANEA: You want to just do what Erik says and give them to—

KAWEHI:	No! I don't want to. Do you?
NANEA:	I want to make a kā'ai.
KAWEHI:	And then?
NANEA:	What were *you* going to do?
KAWEHI:	Find a quiet place—a cave, cool and dry, hidden away.
NANEA:	That sounds like a plan for her.
KAWEHI:	How do you know it's a her?
NANEA:	Because I know. In a woman, the skull is smoother and smaller, the bones of the hands are smaller, and so is the jaw. But the biggest difference is in the pelvic structure. The pelvic girdle is wider, and the surrounding bones more delicate—lighter and slender. If you held the pelvic bones of a woman up to the sky, you would see more blue encircled by a softer whiteness, or more stars framed by their curving arch.
KAWEHI:	You've studied anatomy?
NANEA:	I know a lot about bones.
KAWEHI:	From?
NANEA:	Mostly listening.
KAWEHI:	Are you sure we can do this?
NANEA:	Yes, but we shouldn't tell anyone, not even Erik.
KAWEHI:	He's mad at me anyway.
NANEA:	Why?
KAWEHI:	Nothing.
NANEA:	Can't be nothing.
KAWEHI:	It's the bones.

NANEA: Oh.

KAWEHI: I don't want to talk about it. How shall we start?

NANEA: With 'awa.

(*NANEA stirs the bowl for a moment and looks at KAWEHI.*)

KAWEHI: We're in this together, aren't we?

NANEA: Of course.

KAWEHI: Then you'll swear it as we drink this 'awa that we'll do anything to protect those bones, to make sure they'll rest forever here, where they belong?

NANEA: Do you know what you're—

KAWEHI: (*Raising her voice*) Will you or not?

NANEA: (*Softly, looking right at her*) I will.

(*They drink from an 'awa cup, serving each other. Pause.*)

NANEA: Remember, Kawehi, it was you who bound us together.

KAWEHI: How does it start?

NANEA: Here, at the very beginning, at the bottom of things, at the piko, at the center, the vertical strands radiate out while the horizontal thread makes a continuous spiral, turning over and under, over and under. Can you see? Can you see the center?

KAWEHI: (*Slowly remembering*) You, I saw you. You were in Berlin somewhere. I saw you there.

NANEA: (*Helping herself to 'awa*) It's amazing how 'awa clears the mind, isn't it?

SCENE 15

(*Playing Area. GUSTAV is picking up papers he has dropped on the floor. Enter PUA in the path of the spilled papers. She stops and looks intently at one of them.*)

GUSTAV: Excuse me. I am so clumsy.

PUA: Let me help you.

(*PUA picks up the particular paper and looks at it.*)

PUA: What is this?

GUSTAV: (*Taking it from her*) These are not for. . . .
                   Do you know this woman?

PUA: I'm not sure.

GUSTAV: (*Giving paper back to her*) Look again.

PUA: (*Cagey*) It's possible.

GUSTAV: Really?

PUA: She does look like someone who worked here,
                   maybe.

GUSTAV: Who?

PUA: Why do you want to know?

GUSTAV: Do you work here?

PUA: I'm the assistant director.

GUSTAV: It's a serious matter. Perhaps I should speak
                   to the director first.

PUA: Do you have an appointment?

GUSTAV: No, not yet, I—

PUA: Let me take you to his office. I'm sure if I
                   drew his attention to this, we could see him
                   right away.

GUSTAV: He is a discreet man?

PUA: Sometimes, but he's very careful, and he's into red tape.

GUSTAV: Red tape?

PUA: He never makes any important decisions unless he has at least twenty consultations.

GUSTAV: But this needs immediate action. Very confidential action.

PUA: Maybe you'd like to meet with me first about this in my office.

GUSTAV: I don't know if your authority—

PUA: *(Forcefully)* That woman used to be part of my staff. Do you want to talk to me or not?

SCENE 16

(MINA'S House. MINA looks at a fax and some books.)

MINA: See page sixty-two, *Portraits of 19th Century Hawaiian Chiefs. (Opens book to page.)* Oh my God! *(Looks back at the fax.)* See *Ruling Chiefs*, page 297. *(Opens another book and reads as FATU enters.)*

FATU: *(At the same time)* Mina, you won't believe—

MINA: *(At the same time)* This is incredible—

(Short pause.)

MINA: You first.

FATU: I just saw Gustav, and he's met some woman at the museum. He told her everything. She told him about Kawehi, her address—she painted a very bad picture of her, and even agreed to snoop around for him.

MINA:	Snoop around? Does that mean going to her house?
FATU:	I don't know what it means.
MINA:	What's this woman's name?
FATU:	Pua Hoʻolale.
MINA:	Brooks.
FATU:	What?
MINA:	I know her. She was Kelly Brooks. She changed her name.
FATU:	*(Perplexed)* Kelly Brooks?
MINA:	She's my cousin—distantly, thank god. Like you.
FATU:	Thanks, Mina.
MINA:	Come on, you know I didn't mean it like that.
FATU:	Isn't it interesting how we always end up related?
MINA:	With her, it's not interesting.
FATU:	Sounds like she's got it in for Kawehi. Know why?
MINA:	She's probably in Pua's way.
FATU::	*(Sniffing)* Is that power politics I smell?
MINA:	She screams about injustices done to the Hawaiians, but she'd just as soon bulldoze over a Hawaiian as anybody else if they got in her way.
FATU:	One of a growing number. What do you think she'll do?
MINA:	She capable of anything, and she's smart.
FATU:	If the other woman was really working with him, why would he need Pua?

MINA:	Good point. Speaking of the other woman, your mother sent us another fax.
FATU:	More instructions from the great beyond?
MINA:	References, page numbers. Here, just look at this picture.
FATU:	She's the living image!
MINA:	There's more about her in here, a whole chapter and more.
FATU:	Kuini Liliha.
MINA:	Apparently she was poisoned by a relative.
FATU:	Why?
MINA:	Doesn't say. But it does say that the people loved her immensely, and that if she wanted to, she could have easily rallied them and overthrown the stranglehold of the Christian chiefs.
FATU:	She's lovely, isn't she?
MINA:	She's absolutely magnetic.
FATU:	You said that before about—
MINA:	I did!
FATU:	Do you think she—
MINA:	You mean do I think it could be—
FATU:	No, no—
MINA:	That's crazy—
FATU:	Never.
MINA:	Maybe that salt water and the ti leaves—
FATU:	Stop it, Mina. Don't even think it!
MINA:	We're getting out of control.
FATU:	That's it! It's time for action.

MINA:	Right.
FATU:	We'll take the bones ourselves as soon as we can.

(*Lights out.*)

SCENE 17

(*Kawehi's House. Night. ERIK sits on the couch, moving around some miniature figures on the table. NANEA enters quietly.*)

NANEA:	Erik.
ERIK:	That's me.
NANEA:	You're waiting for Kawehi?
ERIK:	Where is she? Do you know?
NANEA:	She went out with someone I've never seen before.
ERIK:	She does that when she's upset with me.
NANEA:	Why is she upset with you?
ERIK:	Maybe because I'm not Hawaiian.
NANEA:	I don't think so.
ERIK:	No?
NANEA:	It's just things you don't understand yet. (*Looking at figures*) What is that?
ERIK:	Nothing.
NANEA:	Looks like something.
ERIK:	If these were real people, I would be telling them where and when to move around on the stage.
NANEA:	That's the director's job. Arranging the bodies.

ERIK:	You make it sound morbid.
NANEA:	I used to watch them in Germany.
ERIK:	So you've lived in Germany?
NANEA:	Yes, and I liked to watch rehearsals. I know that's not the only thing you do.
ERIK:	Really?
NANEA:	You interpret the script, figure out what's going on in every scene, what the whole play adds up to.
ERIK:	That's us.
NANEA:	*(Sitting by his knees, touching figures)* So what's going on here, Erik?
ERIK:	More than it looks like, I think.
NANEA:	They say the sub-text gives things depth.
ERIK:	They say.
NANEA:	You fight about me.
ERIK:	Yes.
NANEA:	You don't feel comfortable with me.
ERIK:	No.
NANEA:	And you know why, don't you?
ERIK:	Because I find myself drawn to you, like you're pulling at me and I can't stop moving toward you.
NANEA:	And what is it in the through line of action, propelling things forward?
ERIK:	They're under the bed.

(*NANEA rests her head on ERIK'S knee.*)

NANEA:	You will help me, won't you? It's urgent.
ERIK:	What is it?

NANEA:	And it's not just for me.
ERIK:	What do you want?
NANEA:	I want you to take the bones to a safe place.
ERIK:	It's not safe here, is it?
NANEA:	Not anymore. You will, won't you?

(*Pause.*)

ERIK:	We'll exchange them.
NANEA:	Yes, that's it.
ERIK:	I'll take them to the theatre and put the prop bones under the bed. Kawehi won't know.
NANEA:	And she won't be endangered. One more important thing.
ERIK:	What?
NANEA:	Copy the identification number from the bones on the exact spot on the prop.
ERIK:	Where is it?
NANEA:	Left femur. Black numbers written on the bone. That's what they do, assign numbers for the objects.
ERIK:	(*Starts for the bedroom*) I'm going.
NANEA:	(*Gets up*) I'll go too, Erik, so you don't have to be alone.
ERIK:	Thank you.
NANEA:	But you, you have to carry them yourself.

(*Blackout.*)

End ACT I

Act II

SCENE 1

(*Kawehi's House. MINA and FATU, pretending to be journalists, interview KAWEHI.*)

FATU: Right, the *Pacific Performance Journal* is a new scholarly publication.

MINA: Our circulation will be almost exclusively in the Pacific. You know, Hawai'i, New Zealand, Australia, Fiji.

KAWEHI: Sounds great.

FATU: Your role in the production was really unique.

MINA: One we hope other productions will adopt.

FATU: Accurate reproductions, not "props."

KAWEHI: It costs a lot.

MINA: You researched the costumes too, didn't you?

KAWEHI: I did. Of course, we couldn't ask the women to dress authentically.

MINA: You did come close, using body suits.

KAWEHI: Right, and Tahitian camouflage.

FATU:	Pardon me?
MINA:	Long hair, over the chest area. Get it?
FATU:	Got it.
MINA:	Good. Now what about hair?
KAWEHI:	*(Showing them some pictures)* Well, most people have this image of the lovely Hawaiian maiden with long flowing hair, but the earliest artists' drawings we have show women with very short hair and a white kind of lime combed in around the hairline. We couldn't ask actresses to cut their hair so—

(Enter NANEA.)

KAWEHI:	Aloha, you're back.
NANEA:	Aloha kākou.
KAWEHI:	This is Anthony and Kaleinani. My friend, Nanea.
FATU:	Hi.
MINA:	Hi.
NANEA:	Anthony and Kaleinani?
KAWEHI:	They're from the *Pacific Performance Journal,* doing a piece about Erik's production in Berlin.
NANEA:	Is Erik here?
MINA:	We'll be interviewing him this afternoon at the theatre.
FATU:	When we have a look at the reproductions.
MINA:	We heard about the bones.
KAWEHI:	Bones?
FATU:	Complete set, isn't it?

(Pause.)

KAWEHI:	Ask Erik, at the theatre. He'll be glad to show them to you.
NANEA:	They're not there.
KAWEHI:	What?
NANEA:	Didn't Erik tell you? He brought them here last night.
KAWEHI:	Upstairs?
NANEA:	No, right here. He couldn't find room at his place—you know what a pack rat he is—so he put them under your bed for now.

(*NANEA exits.*)

MINA:	Who made them?
KAWEHI:	They were specially ordered from somewhere in Washington, D.C., and very expensive.
FATU:	Authenticity comes at a price these days.

(*Enter NANEA with a bone.*)

NANEA:	(*Waving it around, gives it to FATU*) See? Aren't they wonderful?
FATU:	Like the real thing.
NANEA:	The product of science and art.
MINA:	Perfectly aged.
NANEA:	Distressed, that's what they say in theatre, distressed.
FATU:	Look, there's some sort of number here.
MINA:	I see.
KAWEHI:	(*Thinking fast*) It's a prop code for storage.
NANEA:	Like artifacts.
KAWEHI:	They're being very careful with the reproductions.

NANEA:	Erik's going to pack them up to mail to another theatre.
FATU:	What play will they be in next?
NANEA:	*(Twirling the bone around)* It's a mystery. *Skeletons in the Closet.*
KAWEHI:	*(Inappropriate anger)* Don't do that! You could break it!
MINA:	*(Awkward pause)* Well, thank you, I think that's it for today.
FATU:	Yes, we're very grateful for the time you've given us.
MINA:	Very.
FATU:	And I must say, those bones are a very good reproduction.
MINA:	Excellent.
FATU:	We'll have another chance to talk when we meet with Erik.
MINA:	Yes, thank you, good-bye.

(Exit MINA and FATU. NANEA enters.)

KAWEHI:	How could you do that!??
NANEA:	It's what they wanted.

SCENE 2

(CAMILLA, a refined nineteenth century woman, enters the Playing Area. She spreads a lace tablecloth over one of the tables and places on it a vase with a single rose. She turns to the audience.)

CAMILLA:	January, 1893. My dear Flora, I write to tell you the most thrilling news. I was escorted

last evening to the Bennington Charity Ball by none other than Mr. Warren K. Moorehead—

(Enter to one side a nineteenth century gentleman, WARREN K. MOOREHEAD, attending to his appearance.)

CAMILLA: —the famous collector of artifacts and antiquities for the Peabody Museum and Harvard University. What a dashing figure he cut when I first met him, engaged in serious conversation with Father in the study. I was immediately struck by his dark moustache, his intense eyes which pierced me to the bone, and his general countenance, which oozes adventure, travel, and far off places from every pore. Imagine my surprise when the very next day Father informed me that Mr. Moorehead had requested the honor of escorting me to the charity ball!

(MOOREHEAD approaches the table.)

CAMILLA: He has the most gallant manner, and is ever so modest about his occupation.

MOOREHEAD: I am of course largely self-taught, and the fact is, the selling of antiquities is very tiresome to me—but necessary to support my great passion. Which is field work—the discovery and collection of the objects themselves!

CAMILLA: Mr. Moorehead, I said—

MOOREHEAD: Call me Warren.

CAMILLA: I've read with great interest of your dig in the Ohio Valley for the Chicago Exposition.

MOOREHEAD: Shall we dance?

CAMILLA: He smiled engagingly and swept me away.

(They dance.)

MOOREHEAD:	Ah, yes, the Ohio Valley. I directed a force of men to open graves and village sites along the river, sometimes three hundred feet down. I secured at least thirty-five good crania from that site.
CAMILLA:	Thirty-five! Imagine!
MOOREHEAD:	But at the next site, I really hit pay dirt, as they say. Seventy-nine skeletons!
CAMILLA:	Over one hundred all together!
MOOREHEAD:	And one remarkably preserved child of six or eight years old!
CAMILLA:	What a great contribution to the World Exposition!
MOOREHEAD:	(He leads her back to her seat and stands beside her.) I suppose.
CAMILLA:	You're disappointed?
MOOREHEAD:	No, it's just. . . . I'm sure I should be gratified by my contributions. But you see, my dear, as I said, my greatest rewards are in the field—the strange lure and promise of it all—my joy and drive always boundlessly aroused by what might lie underground. What I might dig up, discover, unbury and expose to the shining light of day—what ancient secrets the earth might yield to me!

(*Exit MOOREHEAD.*)

CAMILLA:	So you see, dear friend, I have quite fallen under the spell of a man of science. Tell me truly, my Flora, do you think I should have any hope of securing the affection of such a brilliant star? Do write me, please do, hurry. All my love, Camilla.

193

SCENE 3

(*Kawehi's House. KAWEHI sits. PUA enters slowly, taking in the place.*)

PUA: I see you still go in for tacky exotic.

KAWEHI: You're not welcome here.

PUA: I think you better listen to me.

KAWEHI: Say what you have to say and get out.

PUA: I met a man from Germany.

KAWEHI: Good for you.

PUA: He told me about the bones.

KAWEHI: I don't know what you're talking about.

PUA: It's no good playing dumb. Have you got them here?

KAWEHI: I'd never tell you what I had here or anywhere else.

PUA: If you don't want any trouble, leave them at the museum for me, and no one will ask any further questions.

KAWEHI: Even if I did have such a thing, which I don't, what makes you think I'd give them to you?

PUA: I'm doing you a favor. I'm helping by negotiating a peaceful settlement.

KAWEHI: Looking for a screen for your other activities?

PUA: There is nothing wrong with my other activities. You make me out to be a monster, but I use my position to help the general welfare of Hawaiians—not some remnants of the past.

KAWEHI: Listen to yourself!

PUA:	We can't eat stones, Kawehi!
KAWEHI:	Can't we?
PUA:	You better think about what you've done. If you're no descendant to those remains, you have no spiritual right to them. I'm a leader in the Hawaiian community. I should take charge of them and—
KAWEHI:	And?
PUA:	And as a cultural authority I can help determine the spiritually correct procedure.
KAWEHI:	Your career, your position—assumed, hired, elected—that doesn't make you a spiritual leader.
PUA:	This is your last chance.
KAWEHI:	That authority comes from another source, Pua.
PUA:	You'll be sorry.
KAWEHI:	Get out of my house.

(*Exit PUA.*)

SCENE 4

(*MINA'S House. MINA and FATU enter.*)

FATU:	(*Tired*) So now we have about fifty pictures of reproduction artifacts and grubby actors.
MINA:	Give them a break. They're in rehearsal.
FATU:	No excuse for slovenly dress, not to mention manners.
MINA:	(*To herself*) Positively medieval.

195

FATU: Did you find the fake bones?

MINA: It was easy. I enraptured a stagehand. We'll get them tomorrow night at the costume party.

FATU: Is it tomorrow? I forgot.

(*MINA fusses with the contents of a box.*)

MINA: I didn't. I found a costume for you.

FATU: That was pretty silly of us to think that Nanea person could have been—well, who we thought.

MINA: It was late. We were tired.

FATU: Did you see the way she tossed those bones around?

MINA: No class.

FATU: And that story about the prop code. That's a museum accession number if I ever saw one.

MINA: Right down to the year of accession.

FATU: They must think we're real fools.

MINA: Well, Fatu, by tomorrow night you will be.

(*MINA pulls out a jester's cap and jingles the bells at FATU.*)

FATU: (*Groans*) I think I hate detective work.

MINA: (*Teasing*) Fatu the fool and his bag of bones.

FATU: Now, now, Mina. "Mend your speech a little, Lest you may mar your fortunes."

MINA: You don't have any fortune.

FATU: Maybe we should go to Kawehi's and switch the bones on the same night.

MINA: Perfect, they'll all be at the party! You know, you should be very grateful I'm letting you wear this costume.

FATU:	Don't tell me, you were going to make me the ass from *Midsummer Night's Dream.*
MINA:	*(Pulls out a donkey head mask)* No! Not you! That part's for Gustav!

SCENE 5

(Kawehi's House. NANEA is dressed like Cleopatra. KAWEHI is in an Elizabethan dress. NANEA pins flowers in KAWEHI'S hair.)

NANEA:	Pass me another pin.
KAWEHI:	I'm not looking forward to this.
NANEA:	Why are you going?
KAWEHI:	I was part of the crew. It would look funny if I didn't. You know, for Erik—
NANEA:	*(Indulgently)* Oh, Erik.
KAWEHI:	*(After a pause)* Do you like him?
NANEA:	Yes, I like Erik.
KAWEHI:	He likes you.
NANEA:	Is that so?
KAWEHI:	He didn't before.
NANEA:	No?
KAWEHI:	He didn't want you staying in my house.
NANEA:	I guess he changed his mind.
KAWEHI:	He can do what ever he wants.
NANEA:	That's right.
KAWEHI:	You can do whatever you want.
NANEA:	I will.

(*Long pause.*)

KAWEHI:	It's all going wrong!
NANEA:	What is?
KAWEHI:	Everything. Maybe I shouldn't have taken them. Maybe I should give them to the museum. Then everything would be all right.
NANEA:	Would it?
KAWEHI:	We'd all be safe.
NANEA:	Except the one who would sit on the shelf.
KAWEHI:	Who?
NANEA:	The person whose spirit is left to wander. 'A'ohe maluhia ka wahine (*The woman has no peace*).
KAWEHI:	But Pua's right. I'm not related. I have no authority.
NANEA:	You don't?
KAWEHI:	You know that.
NANEA:	Maybe you have the highest authority. (*Long pause*) Think back, just think back a little, Kawehi, back to a cold night. It's raining and there's coffee on your breath. You're with Heinrich in the room. You've tricked him, and the thrill of getting away with it is making your heart pound. He leaves the room to get the camera you say you left in his office. You're all alone now, in that room.
KAWEHI:	Yes, I'm all alone and I'm thinking how dark and cold it is all of a sudden. I look around me at the rows and rows of gray steel storage shelves. Aisle after aisle of bones and bones and the words rushing out of nowhere: kupuna kāne, kupuna wahine, nā hulu mamo, *nā lei hiwahiwa* (*grandfather, grand-*

mother, esteemed elders, precious ones), and I feel so lonely, and sad, so isolated in all this chill and gray with the sharp smell of metal and cold, shiny concrete floors. And I'm thinking, how can this be? How can this be real? I look over at one shelf all by itself, with one and only one box on it, and there you are standing next to it, with your arms opened out to me, weeping.

NANEA: Yes.

KAWEHI: And when you put it like that, how could I ever refuse?

NANEA: There was a time when I would have expected more: ritual, veneration, and ceremony. But time goes by and we learn to ask for less. Just a quiet place, cool and dry and smelling of the earth, just a peaceful place to lie, undisturbed, in my own native land. What human right denies us this final resting place?

KAWEHI: After every other insult—

NANEA: What human heart?

KAWEHI: Who are you?

(*NANEA whispers in KAWEHI'S ear.*)

SCENE 6

(*Playing Area, a costume party. NANEA is Cleopatra. FATU is a jester and carries a bag. GUSTAV is in a donkey mask. A WOMAN is dressed as a witch. KAWEHI, ERIK, PUA, and MINA are in Elizabethan garb. All are masked. They dance, and talk in small groups. The party members freeze as three PLAYERS enter, dressed as Elizabethan clowns.*)

PLAYER 1:	What and who have we here?
PLAYER 2:	Judging by their costume, they judge themselves to be fine ladies and gentlemen.
PLAYER 3:	Except the one who perceives himself to be an ass.
PLAYER 1:	A fool.
PLAYER 2:	And she that sees within herself a witch.
PLAYER 3:	What purpose makes them so?
PLAYER 1:	Know not thy betters?
PLAYER 2:	The lords and ladies of this world?
PLAYER 3:	No.
PLAYER 1:	They are actors, Humblebee!
PLAYER 2:	Except when they're asses, witches, or fools.
PLAYER 1:	Which they're known to be with frequency.
PLAYER 3:	What a muddle-brain I am, in this very realm where they "strut and fret their hour."
PLAYER 1:	It is a pity.
PLAYER 2:	Indeed, a pity.
PLAYER 1:	'Tis only an hour.
PLAYER 3:	They seem to know it not.
PLAYER 1:	They must *not* know it, else they would cease to be real!
PLAYER 3:	But they are actors—
PLAYER 2:	So *we* told *thee*, Humblebee.
PLAYER 3:	So you did, so you did. But when their hour is done?
PLAYER 1:	It's off to the bone yard—
PLAYER 2:	Every one.

(*The music comes up quickly as the party continues. PLAYERS join the party. MINA and FATU dance, while PUA and GUSTAV are at a table. The others are engaged in party business.*)

PUA:	Shakespeare was such a racist.
GUSTAV:	White, English, middle class, born around 1564, most likely you are right. But perhaps that's not all he was.
PUA:	Do you have to wear that donkey head?
GUSTAV:	No one must see me.
PUA:	So it's Mina you work with.
GUSTAV:	You know her?
PUA:	We're related, distantly.
GUSTAV:	Everyone here seems to be related.
PUA:	I'm glad to see she's with a local man. No offense to you.
GUSTAV:	He is Samoan.
PUA:	Really?
GUSTAV:	Can I get you a drink?
PUA:	Please.
MINA:	(*Joining PUA*) Pua, I see you've met our friend.
PUA:	Mina, how nice to see you.
MINA:	How are you?
PUA:	Fine. I've been promoted. Yourself? Other than dating Samoans, I mean.
MINA:	Fatu is a close colleague of mine, but I wouldn't hesitate to "date" him.
PUA:	Still no sense of humor?
MINA:	Not like you, coming with a donkey.

(*FATU comes to the table.*)

MINA:	Pua, this is Anthony Lemanatele Fatu. Fatu, this is Pua Hoʻolale.
FATU:	Hi.
PUA:	Aloha kāua.
MINA:	I think I'll help Gustav.
PUA:	Mina tells me you're Samoan.
FATU:	Um-Hm.
PUA:	You know, it's just wonderful how many scholarships there are available now for Pacific Islanders. Especially if you're interested in athletics.
FATU:	Umm-Hmm.
PUA:	Are you?
FATU:	Hmm?
PUA:	Did you ever play football?
FATU:	Well, I played some cricket at Oxford, but when I went to Cambridge, I gave it up. A bit bored, I guess.

(*MINA and GUSTAV return with drinks.*)

GUSTAV:	Here we are.
MINA:	(*Toasting*) Manuia.
FATU:	Soifua.
GUSTAV:	Your father, Fatu. Did you say he was Inspector Fatu, *the* Inspector Fatu?
MINA:	His grandfather.
GUSTAV:	I should have remembered the name when I first heard it. Some of his cases were written up. I read them long ago.
MINA:	I love them.

FATU:	Those accounts were a little romanticized.
GUSTAV:	But the logic, so precise, and such an uncanny understanding of human motives.
PUA:	Does that surprise you?
GUSTAV:	I beg your pardon?
PUA:	Because he was Polynesian?
GUSTAV:	No, I simply admire his work.
FATU:	Come Pua, would you like to dance?
PUA:	It's been a long time.
FATU:	Come on. A lovely woman like you should dance more often.
GUSTAV:	Did I say something wrong?
MINA:	Poor Pua, all she knows is how to attack or defend.
GUSTAV:	Listening to those history talks—I can understand why many of you are angry.
MINA:	Yes, a healthy anger can help us to make changes, but . . .
GUSTAV:	But?
MINA:	But somewhere along the way Pua started to . . . love the taste of her own anger, and it's poisoning her. Will you excuse me?
GUSTAV:	Certainly.

(*MINA exits with FATU'S bag. FATU and PUA return.*)

FATU:	Gustav, you have to dance!
GUSTAV:	I could try.

(*GUSTAV'S donkey head nearly hits FATU.*)

PUA:	Just keep looking to one side.

(*GUSTAV looks, and nearly hits PUA.*)

GUSTAV: Oh yes I see, so I don't hit you.

(*NANEA walks up to FATU.*)

NANEA: Anthony, isn't it?

FATU: Antony, I'm wishing now, to fair Cleopatra.

NANEA: Having a good time?

FATU: Very.

NANEA: I'm going to dance with a beggar.

(*NANEA dances with a player. THE WITCH pokes FATU with her broomstick.*)

WITCH: Don't slouch, boy. A jester should be peppy.

(*FATU stares at the WITCH. KAWEHI walks up to him and gives him a small nosegay.*)

KAWEHI: And pansies, that's for thoughts.

FATU: And what do you think?

KAWEHI: About what?

FATU: Anything.

KAWEHI: I think, I think I've crossed the line where what I think doesn't count for much.

FATU: (*Takes her hand*) I want you to know I—

(*The music gets louder and MINA is at FATU'S side with the bag, whispering in his ear. FATU waves at KAWEHI as he and MINA leave. KAWEHI watches and turns away. The WITCH has been watching also and follows them. ERIK whisks KAWEHI up to dance as lights fade to black.*)

SCENE 7

(*Kawehi's House. The lights are very dim, almost black. Enter MINA with a flashlight. FATU follows with the bag. They are still in their costumes.*)

FATU: I don't like carrying these.

MINA: They're not real, Fatu.

FATU: I don't care. Did you hear something?

MINA: No. Come on. She said they were under the bed.

(*MINA and FATU exit through the bedroom door. The WITCH enters with a flashlight, looks around quickly, and goes into the bedroom. FATU screams and runs back in followed by the WITCH. MINA pauses in the doorway. The WITCH shines her light in FATU'S and MINA'S faces.*)

WITCH: (*Lifting her mask a little*) I knew what you were going to do.

FATU: God damn it! I've told you a thousand times, never sneak up on me!

MINA: (*Kissing her*) Deidre. Not a very warm way to greet your mother, Fatu.

FATU: Sorry, Mother, but you know—

DEIDRE: Save it for later, dear. I'll keep watch. You two finish what you came here for.

(*MINA and FATU exit through the bedroom door and quickly return.*)

DEIDRE: Let's go that way.

(*DEIDRE leads toward the other exit. All of a sudden the flashlights go out and everything is pitch black. NANEA, unseen by the other three, switches the bones.*)

DEIDRE: They both went out at once. Did you see that?

MINA: I can't see a thing.

FATU: I don't like this.

DEIDRE: We need to get out of here.

FATU: I can't get it to work.

DEIDRE: Just feel your way.

FATU: I can't find the bones.

DEIDRE: What?

FATU: I just put them here.

MINA: Ouch, Fatu, you kicked me.

FATU: No I didn't.

DEIDRE: Hurry up.

FATU: I can't find—you didn't have to shove them at me, Mina.

MINA: What?

FATU: God, your hands are cold.

MINA: I didn't even touch you.

(*Flashlights go back on.*)

DEIDRE: You two just get your bums out of here fast!

(*Exit FATU, MINA, and DEIDRE. NANEA sticks her head out of the bedroom doorway and smiles, then retreats. Blackout.*)

SCENE 8

(*Two pools of light in the Playing Area. Two NINETEENTH CENTURY GENTLEMEN step out.*)

DORSEY: Mr. Franz Boas over there is simply sour about me being named Curator of Anthropology at the Field Museum instead of him.

Because of this, he began this personal war with the museum and our department of anthropology, accusing me of things that—

BOAS: *(Germanic accent)* Hardly a war, Mr. Dorsey. As the Curator of Anthropology at the American Museum of Natural History, I would hardly say my actions constitute a war. I was simply saying in that interview that as a collector and an anthropologist, you should hardly presume to put yourself in my league.

DORSEY: Listen, Boas, I have recently collected myself, in the field, two skeletons of the Kootenay tribe, which you could never get because they watch their cemeteries very carefully now. And, I have one complete skeleton of a Tlingit shaman, which is practically unknown, as the Tlingit prefer cremation.

BOAS:: Dorsey, I had already collected and sold many remains to Washington, to Berlin, to important museums throughout Europe before you could even say "anthropological dig," and furthermore, over one hundred and seventy specimens in your own collection are the result of my ingenuity.

DORSEY: Your ingenuity? You mean the Sutton Brothers, to whom you paid $5 a skull and $20 a skeleton.

BOAS: At least they're circumspect. Your paid man Newcombe only knows rip and plunder, chasing epidemics or waiting until villages are out on a hunt to rob their burial grounds.

DORSEY: Oh, you've never done anything of the sort, have you, Boas?

BOAS: At least I have never angered the Indians.

DORSEY No, you let the Suttons do that.

BOAS: You, on the other hand, have actually been arrested for grave desecration.

DORSEY: At least I haven't run a bone brokerage! You're just jealous because your museum's collection will never equal ours!

BOAS: Our collection will equal and outnumber yours.

DORSEY: Not as long as I'm curator of the Field.

BOAS: Better start digging, Dorsey—if you want to keep playing with the big boys.

SCENE 9

(NANEA in her Living History costume in the Playing Area. Separately ,Deidre and Gustav watch.)

NANEA: Boki left Liliha to be his successor in the care of the young king, Kauikeaouli. The boy's attachment to her was very strong, but the Christian chiefs were determined to keep him away from her. They took the king and embarked on a tour of the outer islands to spread the word of God. But taking the boy was not enough. Kaheiheimālie came back to O'ahu and insulted Liliha in public. As the harsh words fell from her mouth, there arose an uproar among the common people who loved Liliha, and were tired of the tyrannical yoke of the Christian chiefs. Talk of rebellion spread, preparations were made for war. Liliha's followers held the port of Honolulu and refused entry to any of the Christian chiefs on the penalty of death. But they tricked her. They sent the one they knew she would never harm—her own father, Hoapili. He persuaded her to stop, and then, to his shame, he watched as those who had sent him stripped her of all land and power. She died sometime later. Poisoned, perhaps by one of her own family. (*Pause*) Few chiefs were ever so loved, were ever shown such affection by the common people. It is said that never has there been, or never shall there be, such lamentations as the night of her death. The river of Kikīhale was stamped dry by the throngs of Hawaiians coming to mourn her in the city. Her body was taken to Lahaina to rest.

(*GUSTAV approaches, clapping.*)

GUSTAV: Thank you. Thank you. I was very much affected. Do you have time tonight?

NANEA: I'll meet you at the cafe. There's someone I have to talk to first.

GUSTAV: Then, I wait for you. Tonight was very special.

(*GUSTAV exits. NANEA approaches DEIDRE.*)

NANEA: I thought perhaps you might come.

DEIDRE: I'm Deidre McIntyre.

NANEA: You mean Deidre Fatu?

DEIDRE: Not professionally.

NANEA: They talk about you all the time in Berlin.

DEIDRE: Really?

NANEA: Mahler hates you. She'd like to see you arrested. She'd die if she found out Fatu was your son.

DEIDRE: I'm careful about that. (*Short pause*) If I had known it would be like this, I would have come sooner.

NANEA: I didn't know myself, until that night when Kawehi came into the room.

DEIDRE: How long do you think it will be?

NANEA: Not much longer, I think.

DEIDRE: Is it hard for you?

NANEA: It should be, shouldn't it? But it's not. I've been watching everything for so long.

DEIDRE: Will you be sorry when . . .

NANEA: No. You see, I'm very tired.

DEIDRE: I understand.

NANEA: Waiting so long.

DEIDRE: I know.

NANEA: I'm worried about her. She's done so much.

DEIDRE: I'll do everything I can for her. That's why we're here. To help her, and you.

NANEA: And the others? There are so many others.

DEIDRE: We're doing everything we can.

NANEA: Tell me, why do you do this?

DEIDRE: I was an anthropologist for a long time. I don't know. I married an islander. My son is Samoan. After a good many years, I just began to see things in a different way. It helps me to sleep at night.

NANEA: I'm grateful.

DEIDRE: Could you tell me how it happened?

NANEA: Well, suppose a person suspected that someone was trying to kill her. Suppose it came to her that she might not have much longer to live, and suppose the one thing that was abhorrent to her was that her bones might lie on the grounds of those who caused her pain and suffering, perhaps even death. Suppose she could not bear to lie on the ground of a Christian god who would never be hers. (*Pause*) There was an old man who greatly loved her and served her, a common man who promised if something happened he would take her away. After her death, he opened the unburied wooden box, and with the help of others who also held her dear, he traded the bodies and nailed it back up. Off he went in his canoe with his beloved aliʻi (*chief*) to a lonely place, where the only voices are in the sea and the birds and the owl at night. There he performed his loving task, cleaning the bones of mortal flesh and oiling them carefully, always in silence but—Auē! Aloha piha ʻo ia (*Oh! He was full of love*). He hid them in a cave and left. No one ever saw him again. They lay there for so long, until one day, foreign men found them by accident. They wrapped them up, took them out, and exchanged them for so much money.

DEIDRE: Then you are whom I thought.

NANEA: How did you know?

DEIDRE: I dreamed of the bones. In the dream a young woman sailed for a far off place in a feather cape. Waving good-bye were crowds. They called out her name.

NANEA: Which was?

DEIDRE: Kuini Liliha.

SCENE 10

(MINA, FATU, PUA, and GUSTAV meet in the Playing Area.)

MINA: I just don't want to be the one who breaks and enters.

GUSTAV: I understand. You two have done so much already.

PUA: You know for sure they're in the house?

FATU: We know exactly where they are in the house.

MINA: And we have a foolproof plan to confuse them.

PUA: Them? I thought they wouldn't be there.

FATU: We're fairly sure she's only part of a larger group, and we think there's a very good chance they're watching the house.

PUA: Highly probable.

MINA: *(To GUSTAV)* Now, Pua drives you to the corner.

FATU: She let's you off here and drives away.

MINA: You enter the house.

FATU: They'll be with us at the theatre doing an interview.

MINA: But make sure the friend isn't there.

GUSTAV: Friend?

MINA: Just make sure no one's there before you go in.

FATU: Take the bones—you'll find them bundled under the bed.

PUA: How do you know?

MINA: We know.

FATU:	Take them to the big empty lot out back.
MINA:	It's overgrown and people have dumped trash there.
FATU:	You'll see an old blue Ford.
MINA:	Go to the car, and you'll see this red sports bag and this bundle in the back seat, identical in size to the bones you took from the house.
FATU:	Listen, now this is very important. Put the bones you have on the floor and then put the bundle that was already in the car into the red sports bag. Lock the car up and leave.
MINA:	Pua will pick you up again at the corner.
GUSTAV:	Clever. Anyone watching will think I have the bones and be led away from the real thing.
MINA:	We wait and retrieve the bones the next day.
GUSTAV:	Excellent, excellent.
FATU:	Then it's over.
GUSTAV:	*(Dejected)* Yes, yes, and back to Germany.
PUA:	How are you going to get the bones back through customs to Germany?
GUSTAV:	Mahler will arrange it all through the consulates.
MINA:	What's the matter?
GUSTAV:	I don't know. It's those history walks. The way she has been explaining everything. I begin to feel very bad about things. *(Pause)* But I suppose I must do my duty.

(GUSTAV stands to exit. PUA gets ready to go.)

FATU:	If anything is strange, just stop and abandon the plan.

213

| GUSTAV: | Until 5 this evening. |
| PUA: | See you then. |

(*Exit PUA and GUSTAV.*)

MINA:	Is the car fixed up?
FATU:	Yes.
MINA:	I hate that part.
FATU:	I'm very careful. I won't detonate unless I know it's safe.
MINA:	If anyone got hurt. . . .
FATU:	There's always a risk, but it's small.
MINA:	I never told you Fatu, but . . . I don't know how to tell you. . . . I really admire you for doing this—these jobs.
FATU:	You do them too.
MINA:	When we have the opportunity, we have the obligation.

SCENE 11

(*Kawehi's House. KAWEHI and LILIHA.*)

LILIHA:	(*Folding up the sennit kāʻai*) It's finished.
KAWEHI:	You did it so quickly.
LILIHA:	We did it.
KAWEHI:	I just watched.
LILIHA:	You helped too.
KAWEHI:	Will it fit?
LILIHA:	Perfectly. But you'll have to finish this one part the way I showed you.

KAWEHI:	Why?
LILIHA:	(*A little nervous*) I have to leave now.
KAWEHI:	When?
LILIHA:	Now.
KAWEHI:	Now!?
LILIHA:	Now—
KAWEHI:	But you can't leave. You have to help me. You have to be here to tell me—
LILIHA:	No.
KAWEHI:	Who will?
LILIHA:	You'll have help.
KAWEHI:	Please, I want you to be here.
LILIHA:	Don't pull on me like that.
KAWEHI:	I'm not.
LILIHA:	With your feelings. It hurts.
KAWEHI:	I just don't want you to go now.
LILIHA:	When then?
KAWEHI:	I don't know.
LILIHA:	You see, the bond is already too strong. It's dangerous.
KAWEHI:	For you?
LILIHA:	For us both. Listen now, and be strong. The ones that were taken keep crying out for home and find no rest. In turn, the islands themselves weep for their return. It's up to you, the living. You carry the past and the future.

(*KAWEHI and LILIHA embrace.*)

LILIHA: Bring us all together and bind us as one, just like we wove the threads together, you and I. Don't cry, and don't fail me. Look what we made. *(Pause)* Here, you should put it away where it's safe.

(KAWEHI takes the kā'ai and exits through the bedroom door.)

LILIHA: Don't cry, ku'ulei *(my darling)*. I'll never be far away.

(Exit LILIHA. Enter KAWEHI. She looks around and sits sadly. Enter ERIK.)

ERIK: Kawehi? What's wrong? I just saw her rush out like the wind.

KAWEHI: Yes, like the wind.

SCENE 12

(MINA'S House. MINA enters with interview equipment and begins putting things away. PUA enters with red sports bag.)

MINA: Pua, did everything go smoothly?

PUA: Like butter.

(Gives her the bag.)

MINA: No problems?

PUA: No. But there's about to be one.

MINA: What's that?

PUA: Yours, not mine.

MINA: Skip the bait, just say it.

PUA: You didn't think I was just going to let that guy take the real bones back to Germany, did you?

MINA:	What?
PUA:	And you, what kind of Hawaiian are you, selling out your own ancestors.
MINA:	This is my job, the way I make a living.
PUA:	Well it's pretty scuzzy.
MINA:	Your place of employment holds a large collection of human remains.
PUA:	This is different.
MINA:	What do you want?
PUA:	By 11:00 tomorrow morning, I want those bones dropped off in a box at the museum addressed to me.
MINA:	You let us find them, get them to a safe place, and then take them for yourself?
PUA:	I helped.
MINA:	What about Gustav?
PUA:	Tell him if he doesn't comply, phones will ring—customs, immigration, police, newspapers, Hawaiian groups . . .
MINA:	I've got the picture.
PUA:	Good.
MINA:	And what do you intend to do with them?
PUA:	First, I'll hold a press conference. Then, I think it would be appropriate to set up a committee to decide what the most correct procedure is spiritually and culturally. We'll decide who should have authority.
MINA:	That could take a long time.
PUA:	What's the rush, once they're back in the proper hands.
MINA:	Germany could press its legal rights.

PUA:	Public legal battles get publicity for issues—
MINA:	And people.
PUA:	*(Exiting)* Just have them there.

(*FATU enters.*)

FATU:	She's not carrying the sunshine, is she?
MINA:	Why does she have to be my cousin?
FATU:	Well, did she—
MINA:	Right on cue, almost exactly like we thought.
FATU:	Like *you* thought.
MINA:	She'll probably show about 11:30.
FATU:	I'll be ready.
MINA:	Gustav?
FATU:	I guess he should be there too. I'll have him drop me off, and tell him to wait down the block. That should be close enough.

SCENE 13

(*A NINETEENTH CENTURY PHYSICIAN enters.*)

PHYSICIAN:	My dear fellow doctor. When I parted with you a month ago, I told you I would send you a present. Well, here it is! A skull, a genuine skull of a Sandwich Islander. It has served my purpose, and now I turn it over to you for, I hope, a place in your outcoming work on crania—a work which I believe will be on the shelf of every man of science for years to come. I give you a brief history of my man Friday. He was about twenty seven or so, and he declared himself a member of a royal line. He had gone out one day on a

fishing excursion and was driven by a storm far out to sea. There he languished many days, when finally he was rescued by a whaling ship and landed near Panama. From there he found his way to New Orleans, and then on to our city, where he fell ill, entered the hospital, and as providence would have it, was placed in my care. He died of nervous exhaustion, and nostalgia. I knew him very well, attended him up to the end, and as he had no means of payment, I made his head responsible for his medical bill. I now place it, a native offering, as they say, on the altar of science—a testament of my belief in the path which I love to follow. Truly, Dr. M.

SCENE 14

(*Kawehi's House. KAWEHI and ERIK.*)

KAWEHI:	(*Distressed*) They were here yesterday!
ERIK:	When we got home?
KAWEHI:	Before we left. I don't check every minute.

(*Knocking on door.*)

MINA:	Hello. Hello. Are you there?
KAWEHI:	We're busy!
MINA:	It's Mina. Kaleinani. Please—
ERIK:	We can't talk now! Go away!
MINA:	I know what's missing!

(*KAWEHI opens the door. MINA enters.*)

KAWEHI:	What is this, Kaleinani, Mina, whatever your name is?

MINA:	Mina. Mina Kaleinani Beckley. I'm helping some people that recover things, unofficially.
ERIK:	*(To himself)* Oh, shit.
MINA:	Don't worry. They're safe, everything's okay. We have them. Fatu, that's Anthony, and I work with his mother on certain cases, like this one, to retrieve things. Things that should go back to their proper places, different things.
KAWEHI:	You didn't have to interfere.
MINA:	Be serious! Germany knew exactly who you were. They would have found you and the bones eventually. We stepped in, because we wanted to get them and other *interested parties*—
KAWEHI:	You mean Pua?
MINA:	—exactly—off the trail forever. Things that don't exist aren't looked for anymore.
KAWEHI:	If it doesn't exist, it's gone, destroyed.
MINA:	No, no, they just *think* it's destroyed, gone, vanished, up in smoke. We took that set of fake bones that Erik locked in the trunk at the theatre—gee Erik, you'd have thought Houdini was in there—and we switched them with the real bones under your bed.
ERIK:	Oh shit!
MINA:	Then, we had Pua and Gustav steal the fake bones from you and hide them in the car we planted in the empty lot.
KAWEHI:	Why?
MINA:	Because in about one minute, that car is going up in smoke and they'll think the bones are lost forever.

ERIK: No, no, you can't do that!

MINA: It's too late. I know they're expensive props, but—

ERIK: NO! NO! YOU DON'T UNDERSTAND! She wanted me, she asked me, she made me —I switched the real bones from under the bed with the prop bones days ago, and now you switched them back! Those are the real bones out there!!!

KAWEHI: No, please, no.

(*KAWEHI runs out the door with ERIK and MINA after her.*)

MINA: Stop! Stop her!

ERIK: Kawehi, no—

FATU: (*Off stage*) Get back! Get away!

(*The sound of an explosion. Flashing lights. Blackout. Lights come up on KAWEHI huddled in the Playing Area.*)

KAWEHI: I don't know exactly how to tell you what happened. It was like watching—just like watching myself in a movie. I was running for the car, and she came, like a fast blurry image out of nowhere. She grabbed on to my shoulders and turned me around and pushed me. I fell forward as if I had been slammed by some incredible force.

(*Lights suggest explosion and fire, no sound.*)

KAWEHI: And then I felt a second push, a lighter shove of air and heat, and in the corners of my eyes the brilliant flash of orange and yellow light, and her body coming over me like a dark wave from behind and falling and the black-ness surrounding me curling and covering me like a deep warm blanket, and things falling all around, hot metal things rushing by.

(*Pause. Enter ERIK.*

KAWEHI: The next thing I know Erik is there, pulling me away.

ERIK: Are you all right?

KAWEHI: Nanea, is she . . . ? Where is she? Did she?

ERIK: She's not here, love. Just be quiet.

KAWEHI: I saw her. She saved me.

ERIK: She's not here, love. She left yesterday morning. Don't you remember?

KAWEHI: I saw her. I did. She saved me.

SCENE 15

(*Kawehi's House. FATU, MINA, and ERIK.*)

FATU: It's my fault.

MINA: No, I'm responsible.

ERIK: I shouldn't have done it.

(*Enter DEIDRE.*)

DEIDRE: This looks like the tomb of gloom. What's the matter? Gustav and Pua weren't convinced?

FATU: Oh, they're convinced.

MINA: Thoroughly.

FATU: The trouble is—

ERIK: So are we.

DEIDRE: Could someone translate for me?

MINA: Deidre, I'm sorry, we blew it.

ERIK: Literally.

FATU: We torched the real bones by mistake.

ERIK: I switched, you switched, and then—

FATU: Poof!

MINA: The ones you have, the ones we got that night, weren't the real ones.

DEIDRE: Yes they were.

FATU: No, Mother, we just explained it to you. They're fake.

DEIDRE: You become increasingly insolent with age, my dear boy. Your mother was an anthropologist in the field for over thirty years. I've worked with bones from New Guinea to China the long way round and back, and I know a human bone from a fake one, thank you.

MINA: What?

FATU: Are you sure?

DEIDRE: Of course I'm sure.

ERIK: But how did they get back?

DEIDRE: That I can't tell you.

MINA: There was something strange that night when we came here. Fatu, you said some weird things.

FATU: I just told you you didn't have to shove the bones at me—

MINA: But I didn't. I didn't touch any bones or you. In fact, I thought you pushed me.

FATU: *(Slowly)* And those hands were so cold.

DEIDRE: Hmm. Well, it wasn't me.

ERIK: Do you think she—I mean who else—

MINA: She must have known—

(*Pause.*)

FATU: Let's not talk about it.

DEIDRE: He has a complex about the supernatural, like Freud.

FATU: (*To MINA*) If I have any complexes, I'm sure they're due to my eccentric upbringing.

DEIDRE: Where is she? Kawehi? The poor child must think—

ERIK: Now I see why, why she did everything—the through line of action. And Kawehi, I didn't know why she was doing what she was doing, until I picked up the bones, until I had to carry them myself.

DEIDRE: Where is Kawehi?

ERIK: She's taking it pretty hard.

DEIDRE: Well don't just sit there, go and tell her!

SCENE 16

(*MINA'S House. GUSTAV waits. FATU and MINA enter.*)

MINA: Gustav.

GUSTAV: I came to say good-bye. You weren't here, so I just . . .

MINA: I'm glad you waited.

FATU: Sorry things didn't work out, Gustav.

MINA: The police say kids hang around the lot, but they don't have any suspects.

GUSTAV: Did you see how fast Pua ran away?

MINA:	I'm sure she's praying no one saw her there.
GUSTAV:	Mahler will not be pleased with me.
FATU:	I hope she doesn't make it hard for you. I'll write her a report myself.
GUSTAV:	You know, in a way I'm glad I didn't have to take those bones away. I mean, I'm sorry for the loss, but after learning a little, I'm glad I didn't have to do it.
MINA:	What would you have done with them?
GUSTAV:	I think, hmm, I think I would entrust them to somebody. Perhaps a woman I met. She gives a history tour in a costume, something I will never forget. In fact, I have her name written here. I was wondering, could you do me the favor of contacting her and saying goodbye for me? She was so kind, and we had many wonderful talks. I won't have time. You could do this?
MINA:	I'll do it myself.
GUSTAV:	Yes, I would give them to her. *(Short pause)* Well, good-bye. You have both been very kind. Aloha, as you say.
MINA:	Auf wiedersehen.
FATU:	Safe journey, my friend.

(*Exit GUSTAV. Silence.*)

FATU:	Feel a little guilty?
MINA:	*(Nods yes)* Umm-Hmm.
FATU:	After we finish, would you like to come to London for a couple of weeks?
MINA:	*(Nods no)* Uh-Uh.
FATU:	Apia?
MINA:	*(Nods yes)* Umm-Hmm.

SCENE 17

(Playing Area. KAWEHI.)

KAWEHI: Deidre, Mina, Fatu, and Erik all helped me to choose a place for her. We picked a night that was bright and beautiful with moonlight, just as she was in life. Together we took her to the home she had waited for, for all these years. Then, we all made a pact of silence. Fatu and his mother returned to London, but pass through here frequently. We agreed not even to discuss things among ourselves, feeling that giving voice to it would somehow be one step toward exposing, would betray that which should be hidden and concealed in the womb of the ʻāina (*land*). But on certain nights, just before I fall asleep, sometimes my room is filled with the unexplainable fragrance of soft blooming flowers, or the fresh smell of the upland forest. I think about her then, to the sound of my own quiet breathing. I think about her resting, and the world gives way to a sleep of peace.

(Playing Area. LILIHA.)

LILIHA: Carefully, carefully, the sennit net draws round to a close. Now carry me far, far up into the hills, and when the air turns sweet, find a place, a small place, clean and dry, inside the cool earth. Lay me there on a bed of green ferns, of palapalai and lauaʻe, and maybe a bit of maile you found along the way. Hide the resting place with rocks and branches, hide it so only the birds know where I am, and then leave me. Leave me in the breathing, beating heart of my beloved ʻāina. I will lie there quietly in the darkness, and in the darkness I will hear them coming.

I will hear the long slow sound of the conch, the steady beat of the pahu (*drum*), and then the creaking of the mānele (*palanquin*), swaying back and forth and back and forth. I will feel their footsteps shaking the air, and stretching out, I will see the endless, winding procession of torches, and then the faces of every loved one gone before me. And one will leave the great line and slowly come toward me, and bending over so softly she calls back, "Stop and wait, for here is one of our own, come home to us at last."

(*Blackout.*)

CURTAIN.